To

From

Copyright

Printed in the United States of America

First Printing, 2015

ISBN-13: 978-1-942022-14-5
ISBN-10: 194202214x

the **B**utterfly Typeface

The Butterfly Typeface Publishing
PO BOX 56193
Little Rock Arkansas 72215

Dedication

Thank you to my daughter April Banks for your support and love – without which, I would not have had the opportunity or time.

Preface

I began to learn how much God loved me and what He made me powerful and capable of on this earth through Him. This was very important to me because my mother deserted me and during that time, no one knew where my father was.

Later, I learned that he had tried to get in touch with me, but was incarcerated at the time. He wrote me letters but I wasn't allowed to read them.

The rest of my family seemed to go out of their way to let me know how *unattractive* I was and that I wasn't smart enough to accomplish anything in life. I was also very shy in school and around other people.

It wasn't until my adult life where I learned that the Word said differently.

I did have a Father, He was a King and He loved me more than I could comprehend. I realized that by birthright, I'm royal. I'm regal! No longer am I ashamed to be me. No longer will I allow people to take advantage of me and treat me any kind of way.

These devotionals came about while meeting with the Lord every day at the same time of day; usually when my grandchildren were at school. During such times, I would keep notes in a journal.

I began sharing the Word of God through text messaging. These messages took off more than I ever imagined. People suggested that I make theses daily devotionals into a book and to that I said, "Yeah ok," but didn't take it seriously – that is until my publisher called the *wrong number* one day and we began to talk about a book. I knew it was God's will that these messages be shared on a broader scale. On top of this, her business was a faith based business! What further proof could I ask for?

God let me know that people understood He is God, but my particular messages were to make people understand who they are in Christ and how to stand tall – 365 days of the year!

May God bless you
with His Word
as it has blessed me!

The Right to be Regal
365 Reasons to Stand Tall

W J Harper

the **Butterfly Typeface**

"Helping to heal the world, one **WORD** *at a time."*

Introduction

If your family members have told you are dumb and will never amount to anything, when you accept this lie into your thought process, it has taken hold on your mind as well as your life. It will then attract those same kinds of thoughts to make itself stronger. Where there is unity, there is strength. Before you know it those strongholds are in your voice, your posture and your eyes.

This is why it is so important to remind yourself that your strength is from the Lord and you are made in His image. The Spirit that dwells within you does not fail.

II Corinthians 10:3-5

*"When a strong man armed keeps
his palace,
his goods are in peace:
But when a stronger than he shall
come upon him,
and overcome him,
he takes from him all his armor
wherein he trusted,
and divides his spoils."*
Luke 11:21-23

Renew

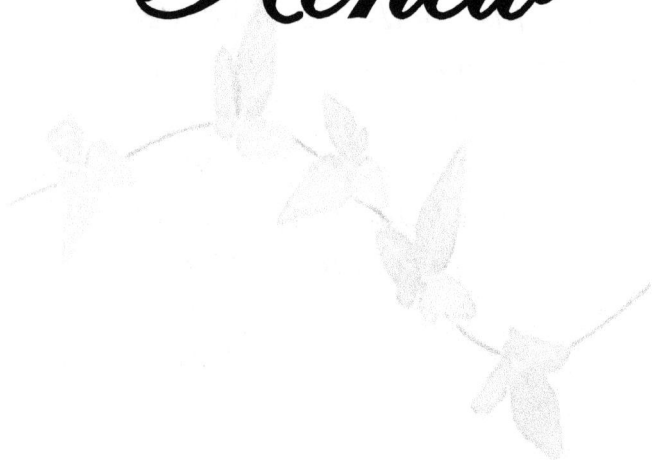

January 1

Psalms 144:3

"What is man that you take knowledge of him?"

Our deepest fear is not that we are inadequate. Our deepest fear is that we ARE powerful beyond measure. It is our light, not our darkness that most frightens us. We ask ourselves, "Who am I to be brilliant, gorgeous, and talented?"

Actually, who are you not be? You are a Child of God. Your playing small does not serve the world. We are liberated from our own fear; our presence automatically liberates others. By: Nelson Mandela

Most of us already know God is Almighty. However, the Lord wants to show His people including myself exactly who we are and why the enemy does not want us to understand. These devotionals are focused on these truths

January 2

Genesis 1:1

"In the beginning God"

Upon opening the Bible God establishes He was here first. Everything else is secondary. Nothing and no one can make this claim and keep a straight face anyway. He does not attempt to explain or apologize for His existence.

When you humble yourself and seek to know Him personally, He will reveal Himself to you.

In difficult circumstances or making life decisions, know two things, He likes to start with **Nothing** and in the Beginning GOD!!!

January 3

Daniel 11:32

"The people that know their God shall be strong and do exploits"

Did hell tremble because you opened your eyes this morning? It should, because it knows that you have potential. Potential to be a spiritual terrorist. You cannot negotiate or reason with a terrorist. Get understanding of who you are. Know that with knowledge comes power. You do not fear darkness. Darkness fears you because it has no choice but to surrender to light.

I pray you get understanding as never before this year through these simple truths the Lord left us to work with. Know your God. It is very important that you realize who you are as well because He lives in you.

The world needs you!

January 4

Matthew 6:25-30

"I tell you do not worry."

Jesus was speaking directly to the Children of God. You see, unless we have been born again, we are only His creations. He said the Gentiles/pagans worry and that your Father in heaven already knows what you are in need of. The only thing worry does is to make us sick.

Studies show worrying related stress is the number one cause of high blood pressure and heart disease. Stress causes veins and arteries to constrict. Therefore, hindering blood flow which causes the blood to backup towards the heart. Worry isn't worth the time and trouble.

Maybe Jesus was on to something.

January 5

Romans 8:1-8

"Not subject to the laws of God, neither can be."

We are to walk after the Spirit of God, not after the flesh. What happens after following the flesh never ends well.

The flesh is like a jelly fish. It has no spine and is carried away by any current. It will not take a stand. It is committed to nothing. It is deceptive, self-centered, loud and suicidal. It is never satisfied.

So let's have a moment of silence for the flesh. Not in reverence but to tell it to SHUT UP! Guard your ear and eye gates. Through them things are submitted to the flesh. If you innocently stumble across a thing, you cannot linger there. The flesh cannot handle such input.

Tired of Satan messing with you? Then leave him alone.

January 6

Matthew 7:24

"I will liken him unto a wise man, which built his house upon a rock."

Position yourself for blessings NOW. Don't wait until something happens before seeking His face. Start building the foundation of your house NOW. It's never too early to pray for children or to find that Godly mate. While you are healthy or before your money dries up, build that relationship with the Lord NOW!

The enemy will try to make you feel too guilty to come to your Father, because you haven't sought after Him lately.

Shut the door and create a time and place just for Him.

January 7

Isaiah 61:3

"To give them beauty for ashes…"

In dealing with ashes, we tend to say Oh well, that's it. It's a rap.

In this verse, the Lord steps in and literally makes something out of nothing. His creativity will amaze you. He has the ability to take our worst losses and turn them into powerful displays of divine beauty.

You'll find yourself after a while saying "Father, you are brilliant."

January 8

Hebrews 11:6

"But without faith it is impossible to please him: because anyone who comes to Him must believe that He exists and that He rewards those who diligently seek Him."

How Do I *please* God?

How do I *get* this Faith?

Romans 10:17 says, *"Faith comes by hearing and hearing by the Word of God"*

Sometimes we need to hear it over and over again before we get it into our spirits before we finally understand it.

So position yourself to hear the Word of God to please him and not be fooled by false prophets.

His sheep know his voice. **(John 10:3)**

January 9

Romans 8:26

"We do not know what we should pray for as we ought, but the Spirit Himself makes intercession for us."

Have you ever decided you were going to pray for an hour, only to find your mind wondering after the first four or five minutes?

The scripture today acknowledges our limitations. We don't know how to pray as we ought. The Holy Spirit helps us by making intercession for us. If we let Him, He will move inside us, stirring up and directing who and what to pray for. It's a holy process. God gave us everything to work with.

Watch your focus change in time as you spend more time with Him. He uses your heavenly language as well. All you need is a hunger and thirst.

Let God use you today.

January 10

Isaiah 26:3

"I will keep him in perfect peace whose mind is stayed on me because he trusts me."

You or someone you know may be experiencing mental illness. When Christians dwell in a land they influence society. The land and people prosper. Studies show they are mentally healthier than any other people in the world. That would be Saints not Ain'ts. The world will not share this fact with you but the Born Again thought process is stable and unique.

The enemy may try to intimidate some by reminding them mental illness runs in their family. However, because of the Blood of Jesus, you and your family are set free to break that curse.

Holy Spirit possess our Thought Life as we renew our minds on a daily basis.

January 11

Ecclesiastes 3:1

"To everything there is a season, and a time to every purpose under heaven. A time to be born and a time to pluck up which is planted."

Maybe today you may be asking "Father, what about me? When will it be my time?" Ask the Lord to show you your purpose.

When it's your season you will be in demand. Doors will open. People will call you. So be prepared. Finish that book, go to school, and perfect those recipes to open that restaurant. Start that trucking company. You may already be prepared. All you need to do now is be still and WAIT!

Know your Father knows the perfect time and place for you.

January 12

John 3:16

*"God so loved the world
that he gave his only begotten son."*

Here we see why God came to earth in the form of man. However, here's something else to meditate on. He came to learn and experience what it is to be a created being by merging with man, creating a totally different kind of species here on earth Son of God/son of man. This is why we need to be born again. Jesus knows our weaknesses and intercedes for us even now.

Can you see why Satan does not want you to know who you are Child of God? You are a totally different species here on earth.

Jesus was and so are you.

January 13

Solomon 5:2

"I sleep, but my heart is awake."

We all get tired and tempted to give up the struggle at times. The remedy is to pray for a fresh out pouring of the Holy Spirit. He knows how to wake us up.

We won't sleep through the war. God is sounding the trumpet, alerting his troops. We are waking up to our great calling as soldiers of the cross the Spirit is winning over the flesh.

Those who have an ear to hear, let them hear.

January 14

Matthew 13:55-58

*"Is not this the carpenter's son... Jesus
answered them, 'Only in his home town
and his own house is a prophet with out honor"
And he did not many miracles there
because of their unbelief."*

Don't get frustrated when you try to share the
Word with family members and get no response.
Some would not hear Jesus either.

Some water, some plant. Your job is to tell them
the Truth. God knows who they are. Only the
Holy Spirit will draw them.

Make sure your witness is not a joke, then put
them in God's hands as you continue to pray for
them, then get some rest.

He will be pleased with you.

January 15

Psalms 16:11

"In thy presence is fullness of joy."

How could God have always been? God is the god of NOW. His presence has always been here. He told Moses "I Am that I AM. As long as there is Now, God will be here. Wherever you are today, remember goodness has always been. Evil on the other hand was born out of hatred for Good and cannot, and will not last. He will never leave you nor forsake you Child of God.

While you are alone, close your eyes for a minute and meditate on your revelation of Him being the God of NOW! He is what He is. Just being natural, supernatural. Just being, a supreme being. Did you feel that? This is the quickening, probably all you can stand. That's how close He is to you. Note: you retreated not Him. NOW is a Holy Place because action takes place HERE. Decisions are made here. You meet Him here. NOW is a powerful place to be. The future can't even exist without it. So seek Him Now!

January 16

Psalms 131:2

*"I have calmed and quieted my soul
like a weaned child with his mother;
like a weaned child is my soul within me."*

A spiritual baby seeks out God for what he can give. As he matures like a natural child with its mother, he seeks Him out for the sheer pleasure and comfort of His presence.

Purpose in your heart to know Him better. He's waiting on you to spend time with Him.

He wants to tell you something.

January 17

Genesis 32:24

"So Jacob left alone…"

To be left alone brings about different emotions. To some loneliness and grief. To others it means rest and quiet. However, to be left alone with God is a taste of heaven.

If His followers spent more time alone with Him, we would have spiritual giants again. In Jacob's case he needed to wrestle with himself and God. He needed deliverance until God blessed him to change his nature.

Our Master often went to be alone with the Father. Make time for Him each day. Maybe a special meeting place where you can be quiet and listen for Him in your prayer closet.

January 18

Joshua 24:15

"And if it seem evil unto you to serve the LORD, choose you this day whom ye will serve... As for me and my house, we will serve the LORD."

CHOICE: Choice is a gift from God. What do you choose today? What God says about you or the world? The kingdom of darkness or the life of the Living God? Letting Him be your Source or unstable mankind? Where will you spend the rest of your day? In truth or in error?

90% of who you are today is the result of past choices.

God made a new day just for you.

So choose wisely!

January 19

Romans 8:1

"There is therefore now no condemnation to them which are in Christ Jesus."

Child of God what you might see as a failure is not necessarily so. In the Kingdom of God, the only way you can fail is to be willfully disobedient to God's will and Word. He will take that dirt and make it fertilizer for your growth.

Know the enemy will take this opportunity to discourage and depress you, but God just wants to know you tried. He loves you. Though uncomfortable, know you are in the right place at the right time. Monitor your choices. Let the Holy Spirit lead and guide you. If He is quiet while in pursuit of Him, continue in that path. He will let you know if you are going the wrong way.

January 20

Psalms 61:2

*"When my heart is overwhelmed,
lead me to the rock that is higher than I."*

FLYING LESSONS:

When it comes to height in the natural, some of us are fearless. Scripture constantly refers to God as upward or higher.

Our base nature interferes with our ability to look up. Notice how hard it is to think positive thoughts. Before we know it we are speaking them. Negative thoughts come easier.

Why? Because we are born in sin. We are naturally afraid of His Higher Presence. Trust Him. He won't let you fall. His thoughts are higher than yours and will carry you and sustain you.

January 21

Daniel 3:17

"Our God whom we serve is able to deliver us from the burning fiery furnace, and he will deliver us out of thine hand."

God does not always give us wings to fly away from problems. Like the three Hebrew boys, he won't turn down the heat, but He will always get in there with you and give you strength to overcome whatever you face.

When you exit you won't even smell like smoke.

January 22

Exodus 16:20

"They harkened not unto Moses;
some of them left of it until the morning,
it bred worms and stank."

Manna was a daily provision. Because God gives
you inspiration about something one day does not
mean it's still relative today. We are to rely on
fresh revelation each day.

If not, human nature will begin worshipping
yesterday's revelation rather than God Himself.
(Another form of idolatry) Just another way to
build an altar to self and making God obsolete. It
will stank in your own nostrils.

Father give us this day our daily BREAD!!!

January 23

Malachi 3:16

*"Then they that feared the Lord spoke often
one to another; and the Lord harkened,
and heard it, and a book of remembrance was
written before him for them
that feared the Lord,
and that thought upon his name."*

Have you ever run into someone and both of you could not stop talking about Him? Believers conversing about God and His goodness brings Him great joy. We know we cannot please Him without faith. We do not spend much time on things we do not believe.

In this verse, Fear equals Reverence. Because they did these things, a book of Remembrance was written for His people.

Speaking about Him in this manner, makes Him smile.

He listens to you as well.

January 24

Hebrews 10:33

"Whilst ye were made a gazing stock both by reproaches and afflictions."

At times the Lord will allow you to be exposed to public insult and persecution. Know you must experience darkness to understand light. Just when hell thought it was over for Jesus, it saw the Glory of God in power and might.

If you are having dark times, know God is using you as a gazing stock. Sometimes, He might hide you before He displays you publicly with power and might.

January 25

Revelation 3:16

"Because thou art lukewarm, and neither cold nor hot, I will spew thee out of my mouth"

This verse says "that taste nasty."

If you are cold, you can at least repent. If you are hot, good! God is pleased! If lukewarm you can not even repent because you have gotten too comfortable to move and will even try to minister to others putting others to sleep as well, maybe even to death.

Rom 3:13 says "their mouth is an open grave." This would make anybody gag.

Let us check our spiritual temperatures today.

January 26

Joshua 24:15

"Choose ye this day whom ye will serve."

THOUGHT PROVOKING HUMOR:

A fence divided a group of people gathering as Jesus and Satan called to them. Everybody chose sides except one man sitting on the fence. Both groups left, leaving him alone.

It was dark when Satan returned. The man asked "Have you lost something? Satan stared at him and whispered "No there you are." The man said "But I sat on the fence choosing neither side. That's okay Satan said. I own the fence. Now let's go.

Once again, what do you choose today?

January 27

Habakkuk 2:2

*"Write the vision and make it plain
that he may run that reads it."*

Just as the word processor has evolved and become more sophisticated, so has this generation of believers. In these last days, you have learned to download needed spiritual data faster. Utilizing the virus scanner (the Word of God), processes and prints out results of your life so that others may read it and run with it.

You are a living epistle (God's Word manifested). You were created for such a time as this.

How's your hard copy reading?

January 28

Ephesians 4:27

"Nor give place to the devil."

This word cautions us to be consistent, trustworthy and loyal to our God, surrendering no ground to the enemy – A hard core militant attitude.

Believer you have the ability to make forward progress without ever loosing ground.

You can be assured that God is at your side fighting with you. For a Believer there is no turning back. You won't fall for old tricks.

Tell the enemy NOT today Silly Rabbit. Tricks are for the spiritually slow!!!

January 29

Isaiah 47:13

"Let your astrologers come forth those stargazers who make monthly predictions, let them save you from what is coming."

You are a new creature. Your sign is the Cross. You are not limited by a star or sign because God who lives in you is not bound by anything.

Don't let anyone curse you by putting you in chains, a box or strongholds again. You are Holy Kings and a Royal Priesthood. Jesus shed blood to set you free.

Some believers try to counteract spells of the enemy by using the same tactics. Not realizing they have joined the condemned to hell.

Why would you want to go backwards?

January 30

Psalms 107:35

"He turneth the wilderness into a standing watersprings."

Don't be sure it was the devil who lured you into the wilderness. Even in those dry places where God is silent he's still watching with a protective eye. Here is where he allows you to blossom into tender desert flowers.

Were you lured there by some other expectation? That person(s) is there to test and grow you. That situation is going to be fruitful.

It's all **Good!**

January 31

Colossians 1:15

*"Who is the image of the invisible God,
the firstborn of every creature."*

How could he be an image of God, if God is
invisible? Once again by His attributes - His
Word. You are also made in His image. So when
God looks at you, He is expecting to see Himself.

What will He see today, ye Holy Mirror? Love,
faith, hope, charity? His power, His might upon
this earth as it is in heaven?

Face to Face: Pray His image reflex in you that
He may see Himself clearly.

Thoughts

February 1

Joshua 24:15

"As for me and my house
we will serve the Lord."

What's up in your house today? Are horror movies residing there? A big picture of the devil and a little one of you? Then you wonder why you and others are hearing voices in your house.

The coffee table is flipping over and you are too scared to investigate so you send your wife. Foul demons riding shotgun in your car through your CD player? At least make them buy gas. Puzzled why you can't get a prayer through? Try doing some house cleaning.

February 2

Isaiah 14:13

"For thou has said in thine heart I will ascend into heaven, I will exalt my throne above the stars (angels) of God...
I will be like the Most High."

Wait! Stop! Hold up! He's going to do what!?

What does **Eph. 2:6** say about you? "And made us sit together in heavenly places in Christ"

I Corinthians 6:3 asks "Know ye not that we shall judge angels" He was going to do what?

Sons of God, Satan hates you because of your eternal destiny. He wants to be you. So leave the eternal looser alone!

February 3

Isaiah 43:13

"I will work and who can hinder or reverse it?
I will exert divine energy on your behalf.
My power is being released.
Your answer is on its way."

Know God's power can flood in on you in such a powerful way that no earthly or devilish force can possibly hold it back.

He might as well try to sweep back an incoming tide with a strand of hair than try to reverse the flow of God's blessings to those He has determined to favor.

Your question has been heard. Your answer is on its way!

February 4

Exodus 27:20

*"Command the children of Israel
to bring thee pure oil beaten for the light,
cause the lamp to burn always."*

Olives had to be pure for perpetual light. God
wanted light in His sanctuary. Olives went in a
giant sleeve and beat until the flesh burst open.

Left to stand awhile, oil oozed out of the catcher,
free of flesh from olives. God does not want to
destroy you. He just wants the product in you.
That product is lessons learned and obedience.

Light in the sanctuary enables one to see clearly.
Know you are the Holy Temple in which He
dwells.

February 5

Isaiah 32:17

"And the work of righteousness shall be peace; and the effect of righteousness quietness and ASSURANCE forever."

How would you live your life if you knew you would never fail and you were always in the right place?

Betcha you would be at peace with yourself and others. You wouldn't have to covet nor fear another. You would watch people fight for position while you looked on with a quiet spirit.

When Jesus went to the cross he **KNEW** something. He had BLESSED ASSURANCE. Actually, you have that same assurance. Because he lives, and you are a Child of God, it's going to work in your favor, FOREVER!!!

February 6

Jeremiah 33:3

"Call unto me, and I will answer thee and show thee great and mighty things, which you do not know."

This verse assures you that if you call on the Lord, he will bring things into the scope of your vision. He will show you great and mighty things that has escaped your attention before with clarity.

He's saying your answer is there. Call me and I will make it visible to you. This includes real motives of people in your sphere. To some, He will show you their true natures in the supernatural realm. You will know who's driving the car.

Questions? Ask Him!

February 7

Leviticus 19:18

"Love thy neighbor as thyself."

The closest relative you have is yourself. How you treat yourself has a lot to do with how you treat others, and how others treat you. If this gives you reason to pause, one or two things could be happening going back generations.

Believing what others say about you or not being connected with your Source which is God. No one can upset you without your permission. No one can prophecy against you without God's permission.

Know peaceful relationships with yourself and others are only a thought away!

February 8

Genesis 3:6

*"And gave also to husband with her;
and he did eat."*

Where was Adam as Eve talked to the snake or the devil? WITH HER! Instead of ordering the devil out, he didn't take his position or authority as head of his household. Influence minus the Holy Spirit can be a dangerous thing.

Ladies a takeover spirit is very destructive. Her household will suffer because things are out of whack. Remember Jezebel?

Take over spirits carry burdens they were not meant to carry. Let him be the head.

February 9

Genesis 2:18

"The Lord God said, "It is not good the man should be alone, I will make him an help mate."

The next few days is for the ladies, discussing her purpose.

Women are versatile. Men generally can only focus on one thing at a time. In a relationship a woman's purpose is to help him and follow him as he follows Christ. However, she cannot follow a parked car.

She births things in the natural and in the spirit. He leads by position; she leads by influence. Together they spell the Power of God.

February 10

II Timothy 3:6

"This kind creep into house and lead silly women captive laden with sin, lead away with diverse lusts. Ever learning and never able to come to the knowledge of the Truth."

This verse talks about women exploited by smooth talkers because she's jealous, needy with low self esteem. All a man has to do is tell her she's pretty. These things make her unstable because she has not taken hold of the Word.

She belongs to the church but never learns. She's the one with the lustful spirit. Her natural gift to gab turns to gossip, she will take up every new religious fad and run with it.

February 11

Proverbs 25:24

"It is better to dwell in a corner of the housetop, than with a brawling woman and in a wide house."

If you have ever heard your neighbors arguing, most likely it is the woman's voice you hear fussing and crying, occasionally you will hear the man's voice grumbling, making a base like sound. This is not sweet music. Most of the time he's not even aware of what he has done.

This does not mean he's right about the situation but the woman has to be wise and pray before dealing with the problem at hand. Because women tend to be more emotional, she needs to quieted her spirit and speak wisely, picking her battles.

February 12

II Corinthians 6:14

"Be ye not unequally yoked together with unbelievers: for what fellowship has righteousness with unrighteousness?"

Single lady, do not conform to this world when seeking a mate. Your faith will be foolishness to him. You don't have to settle.

First sanctify yourself by getting the world out of your system. You are unique and highly valued to your Father in Heaven. So value your time when dealing with people.

Know that men cannot reveal your worth. Know that needy is not attractive. Spend this time alone getting to know your God and yourself and you will attract that special one.

February 13

Proverbs 16:7

"When a man's ways please the Lord, He makes even his enemies to be at peace with him."

When a Christian starts a new job with unbelievers, immediately there is friction or conflict because there can be no natural harmony between light and dark, love and hate, good and evil.

However, it is possible to have perfect peace in the midst of turmoil God is saying here, "Since you please Me, I will cause your enemies to leave you alone. I will also move you or them at the right time."

February 14

Isaiah 54:2

"Enlarge the place of thy tent, and let them stretch forth the curtains of thy habitations: spare not, lengthen thy cords and strengthen thy stakes."

God is speaking of blessings here. But also asks how big is your God?

To enlarge the place, is your mind set. To stretch forth curtains means vision. By faith lift the veil beyond what you can see.

Expect miracles. Dare to Dream big. It is ok to give yourself permission to expand, understanding that the Creative Presence dwells in you.

Strengthen stakes means Stand! Lengthen cords means the Kingdom is topless. Take action by changing your thought process. SPARE NOT - take the limits off your Father.

February 15

Mark 11:23

"Whoever shall say unto this mountain, Be thou removed, and be thou cast into the sea; and shall not doubt in his heart, but shall believe that those things which he saith shall come to pass he shall have whatsoever he saith."

Jesus kept saying speak what you believe. Speak to that mountain. Whatever your mountain may be. Whether health, finances, relationships, etc. You have been given authority to tell it to move.

God does not need very much to help us win. Even if faith is no greater than the size of a mustard seed, mountains will move on your behalf.

Speak to it. It will recognize your voice!

February 16

I Corinthians 1:20

"For all the promises of God in Him are yes and in Him Amen, to the glory of God."

Between promise and manifestation is a place called Patience. Patiently waiting is valuable because God has instruction for you.

While we are waiting, He has our attention. We learn faith, trust, reliance and the power of confessing His promises while learning to follow the Holy Spirit. Just know if God said it, it's a rap. It is done.

Your mountain will move. Amen!

February 17

John 10:10

*"The thief comes only to steal, kill and destroy;
I have come that they may have life and have it
more abundantly."*

We must have a strong sense of ownership to
truly understand this word. You cannot steal
anything that belongs to you already.

All the enemy has in joy, health and wealth
belongs to you. Now walk in this TRUTH, take it
back, you own it sons of God!

Your Father said so.

February 18

Revelation 3:20

"Behold, I stand at the door and knock: If any man hear my voice, and open the door, I will come in and sup with him, and he with me."

When God wants to get your attention, He will not say it once. You will hear that same scripture or ideal until you can't help but notice. They call this the Holy Echo.

Don't ignore the message.

February 19

Proverbs 14:6

"Knowledge is easy to him who understands."

Understand what? God has promised in His Word to make available to His children all the treasures of His wisdom and knowledge if we seek it. Yet we take this powerful promise for granted.

This scripture assures us that knowledge is easy for those who understand the ways of God.

His knowledge becomes your knowledge because you are sharing the same mind. The mind of Christ. You are in partnership together to do great things here on earth.

Once again, set your heart today to know your God!!!

February 20

Deuteronomy 33:29

*"Thine enemies shall be found liars unto thee;
and thou shalt tread upon their high places."*

This word says that truth will be revealed.

Psalms 37:1 tells us not to worry about evildoers.

Psalms 12:13 says "The wicked plotteth against the just, and gnashed upon him with his teeth. The Lord shall laugh at him: for he seeth his day is coming."

The last thing you want is God laughing at you. Only a fool would take this as a challenge.

Don't you lift a finger, for vengeance belongs to Him and He loves you? You are to function from heavenly places.

February 21

Proverbs 23:7

"As he thinks in his heart, so he is."

Thoughts and imaginations good or bad are strongholds. When a thought is given time and meditated on it creates a picture. A thought will produce an image. If someone says the word car, we don't see the word car, we picture a car. The devil speaks to us in images like fear and failure, etc. If he can't give us new images he will resort to old ones, like past failures or guilt. God speaks to you in the Now! In His IMAGE.

Monitor your strongholds. Picture them. Unless what you say is in alignment with what is in your heart, your words will not have any power.

Attach your word with something greater, the WORD of GOD!

February 22

Ephesians 1:21

"Far above all principality and power and might; dominion and every name… not on only this world but in the world to come."

Rejoice and realize God created you a being of strength, ability and power above all circumstances which work for your good.

Others may not know who you are, but the great I AM knows. He knows you have been forgiven by the Blood of Jesus.

This revelation will cause you to begin fixing your own life – a BLESSING going somewhere to happen, moving out and blessing the lives of others.

February 23

Proverbs 13:10

"By pride comes only contention."

Our Pride is usually behind most misunderstandings, disagreements, church squabbles, marital problems, family disputes, etc.

The answer to pride is a good self-imposed dose of humility, instead of the Lord having to administer it.

The Child of God knows that the highest place for anyone to be is at His Feet.

February 24

Mark 9:23

*"If thou canst believe,
all things are possible to him that* believeth."

Do we believe what Jesus said? Know it is possible to believe yourself into a better life.

How can I do that you may ask? Simple, do not let circumstances stop you from believing God because on the other side of your belief are greater miracles than you've ever experienced.

February 25

Deuteronomy 14:2

"Ye are a Holy people unto the Lord thy God, and the Lord has chosen you to be a peculiar people to Himself."

You are a walking contradiction to a lost world. You praise God in the midst of chaos. You are not afraid of the dark – darkness fears you.

The Holy Ghost is your night vision. You pray for those who have wronged you. There are no periods in your life, only eternal comas taking you from glory to glory.

You are only a question mark or peculiar to the walking dead.

February 26

James 1:22

"Be doers of the word, and not hearers only, deceiving your own selves."

Some people are playing themselves, believing they are true Christians. However, in order to carry out their own desires, they will throw God under the bus in a heart beat. It's an easy road to wrong. They bow down but only at the altar of self.

Galatians 6:7 says, "Don't be deceived; God is not mocked"

Let us examine our relationship with our Father today.

The question to ask is this, "Do I have one?"

February 27

Psalms 37:8

"Cease from anger and forsake wrath."

Anger makes us sick.

Maybe you are still nursing past hurts, acts of unkindness and ungratefulness, or other horrific acts inflicted upon you.

I had a problem of being lied on to the point of being consumed. I kept my gaze in the past and mashed on the gas. Until God showed me He always revealed the truth on my behalf.

Anger keeps us blind, sick unfocused, unhappy and backwards.

February 28

Psalms 100:4

"Enter into his gates with thanksgiving and into his courts with praise."

Prayer Week

Let us not forget as a nation, America set aside a special day to thank their God.

This is another reason she has been blessed.

The Bible is very clear how we are to approach God. Come into His presence thankfully. Thanksgiving is the key to the gate. Thanking Him is to magnify Him.

Enlarge Him in your heart because you are big in His.

February Bonus!

Ephesians 4:27

"Nor give place to the devil."

This Word cautions you to be so consistent, trustworthy and loyal to your God that you surrender no ground to the enemy. A hard core militant attitude.

As a believer you have the ability to make forward progress without ever losing ground. You can be assured that God is at your side, fighting with you. For a believer there's no turning back.

You won't fall for old tricks. Tell the enemy NOT today Silly Rabbit. Tricks are for the spiritual Slow!

Thoughts

March 1

Matthew 6:5-6

"When you pray, you should not be as the hypocrites: they love to pray standing in the synagogues and street corners so they can be seen by men. Verily I say to you, they have their reward. When you pray, enter your closet and shut the door, pray in secret, your Father which is unseen will reward you openly."

Jesus is not saying don't pray in public but guard your hearts. Loud speech or eloquent speech does not make a prayer warrior. Speak as you normally do.

If you try to speak all holy or like someone else, your Father probably wouldn't recognize your voice anyway.

Do not be intimidated, BE REAL!

March 2

Prayer Week

Dear Father,

Today, I propose in my heart for you to be manifested in my life for your glory and for others. I wait on you Lord and trust you for you are Wisdom.

I am a willing vessel, excited to see what you are planning for me today. I know all things work together according to your purpose in my life. Like a child, I totally depend on you.

When all is said and done, where else can I go?

March 3

Good morning Lord,

First thank you for all you've done. Thank you for your mercy and patience towards me. I invite you Holy Spirit to teach and guide me.

Open my eyes to anything that may be a hindrance to our relationship. Search my heart and speak to me when my heart wants to doubt.

I declare by faith dead things cannot reside on me or my family anymore. Thank you for moving over their lives with salvation healing and mental stability.

I love you Lord.

March 4

Thank you Father,

As we seek your face this morning, we remember your word says you are a rewarder of those who earnestly seek you.

Let there be a special blessing for those who are standing in the gap for their families. Open doors for them. We know it's your will that our families are delivered from every kind of addiction, depression and loneliness.

We wait expectantly Lord – knowing and believing there is nothing too hard for you.

Holy Spirit continue to move over us.

March 5

Isaiah 65:24

*"And it shall come to pass, that before they call,
I will answer; and while they are speaking,
I will hear."*

Even though this verse is speaking about a new heaven and earth, know that God feels this way even NOW!

He has heard all your heart felt prayers and is working it out for you.

Stand your ground, continue to pray and get out of the way and let Dad do His thing.

Father really does know best!

March 6

Joel 2:28

"I will pour out my spirit on all flesh: and your sons and daughters shall prophesy."

Question your spirit today: "Am I dreaming God's dream or my own? How can I manifest His vision?"

Put yourself in a position to silence the flesh and to hear the voice of God.

A dream or vision is a shutter image of what God wants to manifest here on earth. Images are stored in darkness.

You are carrying around in you a prophetic image that needs to be developed.

HOLY PHOTOGRAPHY!!!

March 7

Prayer

Heavenly Father,

I thank you for providing me even the faith to believe. You are perfection Oh God.

Nothing catches you by surprise, not even when I blow it. Like a loving father you still are merciful and allow me room and time to grow into your image.

I have nothing to offer back to you, so here is my heart, my life, and my will.

March 8

Who is man? What are angels?

In order to answer these questions, you must first *understand* these questions and you need to *understand* your position and theirs: God, man, angels … *in this order*.

Jesus and man are the only ones out of the three who are spirit and physical. God limited even Himself by having to get permission to enter the physical.

Angels are ministering spirits to the heirs of salvation. They are your *servants*. After the fall, a price had to be paid to restore man to his proper position.

Money could not afford you, it cost the Blood!!!

March 9

Mark 9:23

"If you can believe…"

"If we are to live by faith and faith brings answers, why do we need angels?"

Because learning to live by faith is a process. You don't decide today, then tomorrow you are a pro. The word has to be planted in you, watered and cultivated until your due season.

Meanwhile, you may encounter an emergency or problem you have not developed the faith for. This is when you need angels to get involved in your lives. They are the mercy of God.

March 10

Matthew 26:53

*"Think I cannot now pray to my Father,
and he shall give me
more than 12 legions of angels now?"*

There are 6,000 men in a Roman legion.

Jesus said He could call up MORE than 12 legions of angels if he wanted to. 12 legions equal 72,000 angels. One angel is far more capable and powerful than anything we could imagine.

Being God/man, Jesus spoke from his humanity.

If you are a child of God, you too may call upon these angels.

I love you so much Jesus!

March 11

Romans 8:29

"For whom he did foreknow he also predestined to be conformed to the image of his Son, that he might be the firstborn among many brethren."

Think back you have encountered an angel on your behalf. When your mind was not on the Lord, events happened in your life you know it was divine intervention. Narrow escapes, people died but you lived. Plans to harm you but saw a big man or men behind you. Despite your plans you were predestined to be like your big brother Jesus.

Remember He said you would do even greater things than Him.

You are among many brethren so don't hesitate to call upon God's ministering spirits for help. Just make sure they belong to God.

March 12

Psalms 34:7

"The angel of the Lord encamps around about them that fear him and delivers them."

There is no set formula for angelic assistance but there was a pattern among those in The Bible who did receive help. It was LIFE STYLE. A common attitude about life. A fear of God. They sought out the Word of God, Repentance then Prayer.

They always prepared to be blessed. This does not mean we can arrogantly order them around. They get their orders from God.

March 13

Luke 10:19

*"Behold, I give you power to tread on serpents
and scorpions and over All the power
of the enemy and NOTHING shall
by any means hurt you."*

Knowledge of authority affects both good and bad angels. They understand authority better than us humans. Not understanding the finished work of Christ is the problem.

Satan is believing that he is in a higher position when in fact, he's under our feet.

Evil spirits know if we are operating in the word of God or not.

March 14

Acts 15:29

"Abstain from meats offered to idols and from blood and from things strangled."

God gave specific instructions on killing animals for consumption. This is called Kosher.

They kill the beast with a knife that must be razor sharp. A silk cloth is run across the cutting edge. If the knife snags, the knife must be repaired or replaced. The koshering Rabbi then approaches the animal from behind and slits its throat so the animal experiences **No Fear**.

Slaughter techniques that cause fear in animals causes unnatural high amounts of hormones and other disturbing results.

Stress is no good under any circumstances. You as a believer are to seek first the kingdom of God. He promised peace to those whose minds are stayed on Him.

March 15

II Timothy 1:7

"God has not given us the spirit of fear."

The first reaction after eating of The Tree of Knowledge was fear. They ran from God. It's amazing how much fear is at the bottom of evil and worry. Jealousy, fear someone will get ahead of us or we are missing out on something.

This is how Satan got Eve to listen to him. She thought she was missing something she already possessed.

We stay in abusive relationships, fearing we can't do any better or fear we have displeased God in someway in the past and He will not forgive us. Maybe bad reports.

Check your actions and worries today and see what comes up or what's at the bottom of such worries.

If it is fear, make it bow down once and for all.

March 16

Genesis 17:1

"I am Almighty God."

When thinking of the word masculine: strength leadership, protector, provider and sustainer comes to mind. These things most men strive to be naturally.

They are the family covering. But who covers you when you need comfort and direction? Know it is **El Shaddai**, the Blessed One or Almighty God. Out of all His names, this explains His nurturing nature.

Everything you need to survive emotionally. He provides for you, minus the mood swings.

March 17

II Corinthians 12:10

"When I am weak, then I am strong."

Men are wired to lead and conquer, but forget sometimes where their strength comes from, finding it weak to seek help, even when saved. You see this in churches where membership is predominately female.

Women know how to surrender and receive. Seek Him and recognize your dependence on the Lord and recognize your dependence on Him.

Ask questions. Asking shows humility and dependency on your God. Ask Him to show you how to pray. Command your soul to bow down and know true strength and PEACE!

March 18

I Peter 5:8

"Your adversary the devil, as a roaring lion walks about seeking whom he may devour."

Men, the previous message exposed your enemy and gave you ammunition and direction on how to protect yourselves and your loved ones by being the head in your households, leading and guiding by examples. Some of you were sucker punched. Your enemy told you that couldn't happen in your home it will never change.

They will think I am weird. News Flash, they already think you're weird, or "they know my walk is shaky"

Good News. Today is a New Day. It may be awkward at first but in time they will love and respect you for it.

March 19

Proverbs 18:22

"Whosoever finds a wife finds a good thing and obtains favor of the LORD."

Single Men: FMSM (Feed My Sheep Ministry) surveyed a few men of every age range, saved and unsaved, single and married regarding their ideal woman.

The general consensus besides the obvious were: clean, able to interact socially but not loud and appreciative.

On the last one, even God wants to be appreciated. These things are fair.

Before choosing your special someone make sure she has these qualities, but above all she should love God your Father.

However, remember she has the right to expect the same from you.

March 20

Proverbs 18:10

"The name of the Lord is a strong tower; the righteous run into it and is safe."

For the next few days we will be discussing the names of God.

In biblical days a name represented a person's character. To boast in His name is to have confidence in who He is. His names provoke hope and strengthens our faith.

If your heart is troubled in any way, write it down then take it to Him in the name that fits your situation.

When He shows you, tell Him you will boast in that name.

March 21

Romans 8:28

"We know all things work together for good to them that love God, to them called according to His purpose."

El Roi means the God who sees. Whether you were treated unjustly, lied on or deep down in your heart you ask "Did I fail in some way? If I had handled that differently the result would be better" Remember your God saw the whole thing.

Trust *El Roi* to work it out for your good. Because you love Him He uses every situation to grow and bless you.

March 22

Psalms 9:10

"They that know thy name
will put their trust in thee: for thou,
Lord has not forsaken them that seek thee."

If you have loved ones who have run away or on drugs, *El Roi* know and sees them. Run into the strong tower of his name and rest.

This truth will be your comfort, healing, sanity, hope and protection. **Psalms 139:7-12** says, "Where can I go from thy Spirit? Or where can I flee thy presence?"

God knows exactly what to do and to show up on your behalf."

March 23

Luke 6:46

*"Why do you call Me, Lord, Lord;
and do not what I say?"*

Before we can benefit from the rest of God's
names we must know and understand the name
Adoni. Lord ***Adoni*** indicates a relationship. His
total procession of you, and your total
submission to Him as Lord and Master.

We need to think again before we say, I know
what the Word says, "BUT." To know Him as
Adoni, we might want to bow in our spirits and
get our BUTs out of the way.

March 24

Isaiah 14:24-27

"...the Lord of host has planned and who can frustrate it? And as for His stretched out hand, who can turn it back?"

El Elyon means the Most High, sovereign ruler of the universe. If God is not sovereign, He is not in control. If all things are not under His domain, then He is not the *Most High* and you and I are either in the hands of fate, man or the devil.

Thank God we have options. Know nothing can separate you from the love of God.

Choose *El Elyon*.

March 25

Exodus 3:13-14

"They shall say to me, "What is His name?"
What shall I say to them? God said to Moses.
I AM THAT I AM.
Say to the children of Israel,
I AM has sent me."

Jehovah means the unchanging God. When you accepted Jesus into your life, promises were given to you as a child of God. He refers to us as His covenant people. Promises and Mercy gather around the name of Jehovah.

He was there, keeping His promises, even in times when you didn't keep yours.

His name won't change because He can not change.

March 26

Genesis 22:8

"Abraham said my son,
God will provide himself
a lamb for a burnt offering."

Jehovah Jireh means the Lord will PROVIDE. Did Abraham say this in faith or he didn't want to scare his son?

Scripture is not clear, but Jehovah shows us the very essence of God is love. He desires to meet the needs of those created in His image. To be beyond Himself is part of His character.

As we take on His character, we reach out beyond ourselves, revealing His character which reveals His true nature here on earth.

To be continued

March 27

Genesis 22:8

"Abraham said my son,
God will provide himself
a lamb for a burnt offering."

Abraham and his son saying that it was by faith he answered him the way he did, but it still does not say what he was thinking. Obviously he had faith because he told the men with him they both would return.

Maybe he thought if he killed him, God would resurrect him or cause the knife not to hurt him.

The point is he was obedient. God had made a covenant regarding Isaac in **Genesis 17:19**. Know if *Jehovah Jireh* promises, He will provide all the details.

Our job is to TRUST in Him.

March 28

John 3:16

*"God so loved the world
that he gave his only begotten Son."*

Is it arrogant of humans to feel they are the only ones in the universe?

John 3:16 says Jesus was His only begotten, meaning God never shared His divine nature with any other creature, be it angels, Martians or animals.

So human blood was required. Satan wants you to constantly question your identity.

Jehovah Jireh gave that you would be part of Him.

Know God + you = Majority.

March 29

Isaiah 26:3

*"Thou wilt keep him in perfect peace
whose mind is stayed on thee."*

Jehovah Shalom means the Lord is PEACE.
Seems man will not appreciate the peace of God
until the hour is dark and desperate.

But when fear grips us, insanity is at the door we
seek security that everything will be alright. Yet
fear that comes from life is nothing compared to
finding oneself face to face with God Himself.

The TRUTH the Prince of Peace assures us is
sound minds and calm souls.

March 30

I Samuel 15:1-3

"Now go and strike Amalek and utterly destroy
all he has do not spare him;
but put to death both man and woman,
child and infant, ox and sheep,
camel and donkey."

Wow God! Really? Everything and everybody?

Jehovah Nissi means the Lord is my Banner meaning the flag or banner which went before an army boasting and representing.

Amalek is a type of flesh. The flesh is a mindset, an enemy of God who cannot be tolerated, catered to or spared at any time. Eventually the flesh will yield more fruit.

God first = VICTORY

March 31

Galatians 5:24

"Those who belong to Jesus have crucified the flesh with its passions and desires."

Death to the flesh should be the goal of believers.

Why?

If you don't declare the flesh dead, it will eventually humiliate and kill you.

Instead of destroying Agag, king of the Amalekites, Saul brought him back captive, only to become the captive of an Amalekite and die by his hand.

Agag was Esau's grandson who gave up his birth right for a bowl of stew.

IS IT WORTH IT?

Thoughts

Rejoice

April 1

Hebrews 10:10-14

"We have been sanctified through the offering of the body of Jesus Christ once and for all."

Jehovah Maccaddeshcem means the Lord sanctifies you meaning set apart. Good News you are not at the mercy of some god who might be on one today, wanting you to jump into a fire and throw your kids in too. Instead He became the sacrifice.

Flirting with Christianity? Or do you love God with all your heart, mind and strength?

April 2

John 15:5

"I am the vine, ye are the branches: He abideth in me and I in him, the same brings forth much fruit: for without me ye can do nothing."

Know this if nothing else: Only by abiding under the power, banner of your *Jehovah Nissi* can you overcome the flesh, the world, your tongue, thought life, the devil, your enemies and God's enemies.

He says the battle is His. Trying in your own strength will result in beat-downs one way or the other.

As for the flesh, LET IT GO MAN!

April 3

John 10:26

"Ye believe not believe you are not my sheep...
My sheep hear my voice and know my voice and
I know them and they follow me."

God refers to us as sheep. Sheep are dumb animals. Therefore, they are helpless, timid, and feeble minded requiring constant attention and care of a shepherd.

Jehovah Rohi means the Lord my Shepherd. The difference is sheep depend on the shepherd. Do we need a shepherd? Think back on all the dumb stuff you did. Then have mercy on new believers.

April 4

Psalms 23:1

"The Lord is my shepherd. I shall not want."

Sheep without shepherds go wrong ways unaware of danger. Without shepherds to lead them to new pasture, they will nibble themselves off a mountain side, eat or drink things harmful to them. They will live their lives in a rut and die in a state of panic and depression. They fall prey to predators without the shepherd's protection.

As G. Craige Lewis might say, thank you Lord for deliverance from the 'Spirit of Dumb.'

April 5

Psalms 138:2

"For thou hast magnified thy word above all thy name."

As your Shepherd, His reputation is at stake. So He cannot fail. His word stands because he places it above His own name.

Sheep cannot lay down as long as they are hungry. The Shepherd so satisfies their hunger they can lie down in the midst of green pastures.

Fear keeps them awake. Friction with their own kind will keep them on their feet.

Jehovah Rohi watches His own.

Shut up, Look Up and Rest!

April 6

John 10:3

"He that enter in by the door is the Shepherd. To him the porter open and the sheep hear his voice and he calls his own by name."

So why do some prefer to draw back, and close themselves off from Christ, feeling safe, in self made prisons?

Most of the time it's trust issues. They have encountered a thief and robber of TRUTH. But the porter who opens the door for the Shepherd is the Holy Spirit who comes lovingly and quietly to begin His gentle work in you.

April 7

Proverbs 8:17

"I love them that love me and those who seek me early shall find me."

The Shepherd gets up early leading his sheep out of the pen because it is only for their protection at night. It is filthy because they had to do their business in that spot and there is no food. They are lead out to graze peacefully on moist vegetation.

The best time for prayer is early in the morning. This is when you are fresh, and spend quiet time with the Master while the most of the world is still sleeping

April 8

John 10:10

*"I am come that they might have life,
and they have it more abundantly."*

Jehovah Rohi gave His best "HIMSELF" He is not way out there somewhere. He completely enfolds and surrounds you with His presence. The life of God given to men is the same life that fuels the cosmos and sustains the universe.

The best a mere mortal can do is quietly go somewhere alone and meditate on His splendor and abundance and try to grasp the fact that He loves you sooo much.

He's more than a good shepherd, He is the **Shepherd**.

April 9

Psalms 139:1

"Lord, thou has searched me and known me."

A shepherd will watch carefully as each sheep comes through the gate. Everyday he will speak to his favorite in endearing terms, examining and scrutinizing, checking to see if all is well. They sense they are safe and assured by his embrace.

It is important for your relationship with the Lord to know he watches and will anoint your head with oil to rid you of pestilence.

Oil = the Word of God.
Pestilence = tormenting thoughts and lies.

April 10

Hebrews 4:7

*"Today if ye will hear his voice,
harden not your hearts."*

It is almost embarrassing how much our behavior patterns are like sheep. It is frustrating to the shepherd when he calls his sheep and a few stand there stubborn and stupidly waggling their ears and bleating Bah!

They are usually the ones who wonder off in all kinds of danger and self destruction.

The ones who follow Jesus find comfort and are exposed to new experiences and adventures.

April 11

Matthew 11:28

"Come to me, all ye that labor and that are heavy laden, and I will give you rest."

Judge the Shepherd by his sheep. God's sheep are marked. As long as they are under his care they have restful spirits about them.

Those who live in this serene communion with Christ know they are in His hand and will not be moved. The secret is not trying to hold onto Him doubting your own feeble efforts but to rest in any situation.

This may take some time but know He is working it all out for your good.

April 12

Hebrews 10:4

"It is not possible the blood of bull and goats can take away sins."

Animal blood cannot take away sin because the problem is the heart. We could never be righteous on our own.

Psalms says the heart is desperately wicked. Now what?

Jehovah Tsidkenu means the Lord our Righteousness. He promised "I will put My law within them and on their heart I will write... I will remember their sin no more... I will put my Spirit within you and cause you to walk in My statues.

We are without excuse!

April 13

Exodus 13:20-22

"He did not take away the pillar of cloud by day, nor the pillar of fire by night from the people."

Jehovah Shammah means the Lord is THERE! As He led the children of Israel He never took a break night or day.

Know you are Holy Ground because the Lord lives inside you day and night.

Psalms 132:8, 13-14 says "This is my resting place forever; here I will dwell, for I have desired it. Note your adversary hopes you move so you will become easy prey.

But He is THERE!

April 14

I Corinthians 3:16

"Know ye not ye are the temple of God and the Spirit of God dwells in you."

The **Shekinah** Glory means the manifest Presence of God. That same glory that tore open the curtain of the Holiest of Holies resides in you.

Jeremiah 31:31-33 says, "Let them make me a sanctuary that I may dwell among them. God's ultimate goal has always been to dwell in us. When you accepted Jesus Christ, **Jehovah Shammah** is there for you and in you to become God's manifest presence here on earth.

April 15

Jeremiah 8:22

"Is there no physician there"
Is there no balm in Gilead?"

Yes, there is a balm in Gilead and a physician. His name is *Jehovah Rapha* meaning the Lord that heals.

He heals everything that is sick: Physical illness, mental illness, the soul, the broken hearted, demon possessed, even nations.

Trust and believe *Jehovah Rapha* is capable of healing anything that's not right.

Pray that our nation does right by Israel regarding Egypt.

April 16

Psalms 103:2-3

*"Bless the Lord, O my soul and
forget not all His benefits:
Who forgive ALL thine iniquities;
who heals all thy disease."*

Although not always the case, sin affects man's spirit, and the spirit can cause sickness of our emotions and body.

God always meets us at the point of our obedience and there when we head towards Him.

Note: **Psalms 103:3** "pardons all your inequities" comes before "healing all your diseases"

If you need healing, check this fact out first.

April 17

Exodus 15:26

"If you listen carefully to the voice of the Lord your God and do what is right in His eyes, if you pay attention to His commands and keep all His decrees, I will not bring on you any of the diseases I brought on the Egyptians, for I am the Lord who heals you."

There is a difference between falling into sin and out right practicing sin. None of us are perfect. So don't let the enemy convince you God won't heal you because you have made mistakes.

April 18

Jeremiah 6:63

*"The words I have spoken to you are spirit
and they are life. Yet there are some
who do not believe."*

God's word contains healing power. If He says "I
am the God that heals thee, you best to believe
He can and will.

Find a healing scripture then continue to speak it
until your spirit receives it and you are healed.

If you have to take medication, with each pill
confess with your mouth "By His stripes I am
healed." Let us put some feet to our faith, never
giving up!

April 19

Matthew 6:10

"Thy Kingdom come. Thy will be done in earth, as it is in heaven."

As the WORD walked the earth he healed the sick and cast out devils. He said he did what he saw his Father do. Question: Is there any illness, ghettos or demons in heaven? Know it is God's will for you to be healed as long as you are assigned to this earth.

Ephesians 2:6 says, "We sit in heavenly places in Christ Jesus."

Tell your body this: "We declare our bodies, wombs and families healthy on earth as they are in heaven."

SPEAK and PRAY His WORD!

April 20

Luke 18:1

"Men ought to pray and not faint."

Attention spans can be very short when praying for healing, etc. We want to confess the word a couple of times, then say it's not working, switching back to devil speak, "Guess I just have to deal with it, after all we're all going to die of something"

Is your body the temple of God? Does *Jehovah Rapha* get the glory here on earth from living in a broke down shack? How will they know Him?

Speak to that mountain.

April 21

Acts 4:12

"Salvation is found in no other name under heaven given to men whereby we must be saved."

This is the last name - *Jehovah My Salvation.*

At the name of Jesus, everybody and everything must bow.

This name was given to you for salvation, illness, demons, finances, etc. Every series on healing I get blessed personally because He is REAL!

Some good resources on sheep and healing are Phillip Keller's, "A Shepherd Looks at Psalms 23" and "Christ the Healer" by F.F. Bosworth.

April 22

James 1:3-4

"When your faith is tested,
your endurance has a chance to grow.
When your endurance is fully developed
you will be strong in character
and ready for anything."

Ever had days when you were so overwhelmed you just wanted to sleep all day? God seemed to ignore you?

Next time go back. Back to the time He came through for you. Build an altar THERE.

Your problems are making you stronger but when He brings you through this time, give thanks to Him, giving Him the glory THERE!

April 23

Psalms 99:1

"He dwells between the cherubim."

The mercy seat protected man from God's judgment represented by the judgment angels facing each other on the ark. Because blood sprinkled on the mercy seat, man's guilt was washed away and the curse of the law ineffective.

Jesus is our mercy seat and forever stands between a holy God and sinful man.

Do not let Satan torment you by rehearsing the past. He is defeated forever. Apply the blood of Jesus on your conscious and move on.

April 24

Philippians 4:13

"I can do all things
through Christ who strengthens me."

Jesus promised a Comforter but just before His
ascension he also promised the power of the
Holy Ghost. Power for what? Power to witness,
overcome, etc.

We may gaze at jets or new technology and are
amazed and say look what man has done.

However, that's what man does without God.
Watch what he can do with GOD. He wants to
give you a view from the top of life and see what
He sees.

April 25

Hebrews 11:16

"Now they desire a better country, that is, an heavenly one; wherefore God is not ashamed to be called their God for he has prepared for them a city."

TEENAGERS:

When you were born again, your citizenship changed. You are no longer of this world but born from above.

You speak a different language than the world. You speak with an accent from another kingdom. They hear foolishness.

Be encouraged. You were chosen from the foundation of the world and never meant to fit in. God is proud of you. STAND!!!

April 26

Matthew 10:16

"I send you forth as sheep in the midst of wolves; therefore be wise as serpents, and harmless as doves."

My Teenagers, you are called to greatness and as stated before you are bi-lingual in this world. You have a kingdom accent. But different does not mean to be weird. Too heavenly minded to be any earthly good. **II Corinthians 5:20** says, "You are ambassadors for Christ."

So display your country with wisdom, joy and victory. Watch your life become a magnet.

April 27

II Timothy 2:4

"No man that wars entangles himself with the affairs of this life; that he may please him who has chosen him to be a soldier."

Soldiers always come with orders. God's army is no place for wimps. Wimps whine and complain, blaming everybody but themselves why they will not obey God's orders.

Then when life hits the fan, the hard core start screaming like little girls. So let's stand men and women of God.

Fight the fight of faith, when life goes Boo!

April 28

Ephesians 6:16

*"Above all, **taking the shield of faith,
wherewith ye shall be able to quench
all the fiery darts of the wicked.***"*

In Roman days the shield was as big as a door. With it a soldier could advance under attack knowing that he had no area exposed.

Fiery darts are lies of the enemy. Learn to 'word' Bang!

No area of your life can be touched with the shield of faith. It completely covers every area of your existence. It not only protects but gains ground against the enemy.

Our war cry is YES LORD!!

April 29

II Corinthians 10:4

"The weapons of our warfare are not cot carnal but MIGHTY through God."

Yes, we're still Word Bangin. The messages have been aggressive and militant. The enemy is no joke but neither is our Father. If he gets in your face saying you are defeated, weak, ill, broke and dumb, do as Jesus did. Speak the Word back to him. You are not dumb you have the mind of Christ.

God wants you healed. Jesus died so you would have abundant life. The TRUTH.

Knock him out warriors!

April 30

Luke 6:48

*"Like a man who built a house deep
and laid the foundation on a rock and when the
flood rose the storm beat vehemently upon the
house and could not shake it:
for it was founded upon a rock."*

The Rock is the Word which is the truth. The wise man did not wait until something happened to believe. He dug deep until he found the foundation.

If trouble comes your way, be prepared. Have that Word so embedded in you that you can't and won't be shaken or moved.

That situation will have to move instead!

Thoughts

May 1

Good morning Lord,

Thank you for your presence and mercy in my life. Thank you for my anticipated healing and prosperity for your glory.

Lord I seek your face, hungering to know you more and more each day. Holy Spirit continue to be the light which opens my eyes. Because of you Father, I fear no evil report. I need to tell you, just needed to tell you, I love you with all my heart!

Signed,

Your Child

May 2

John 17:16-17

*"They are not of this world,
even as I am not this world."*

"Sanctify them through thy TRUTH:"

Sanctify = Holy and set apart.

Child of God, the TRUTH sets you apart from the world. You are not comfortable with the things of this world. Know you make them nervous as well. Upon creation, one of the first things God did was to separate light from dark.

Don't forget *I Peter 2:9* says we too were called out of darkness into his marvelous light.

In fact, you are the Light of the world!

May 3

Matthew 18:19

*"If two of you agree on earth as touching
anything they ask it will be done
for them of my Father."*

We know the earth all spoke one language at
some time in history and the Lord intervened,
because He said anything would be possible to
them.

The problem was they were agreeing to do evil,
not led by His Spirit. Now Jesus says agree with
someone in His name and it will be done.
Imagine thousands of people praying on one
accord.

Careful what you agree upon whether serious or
jokingly. Let us pray for our brothers and sisters,
being persecuted all over the world right now.

There is power in AGREEMENT!

May 4

Psalms 61:2

"When my heart is overwhelmed,
lead me to the rock that is higher than I."

Let me tell you about yourself. David's heart was overwhelmed but acknowledged that God was higher than him or any circumstance.

Careful, fretting and worrying can come under the heading of exaltation of self. You may find yourself worshipping at the altar of "I.".

Self is incapable of loving anyone but self. Self will turn on self, then try to prove self.

Seek the Rock that is higher than you!

May 5

Psalms 61:2

"When my heart is overwhelmed,
lead me to the rock that is higher than I."

This walk requires that we die to self. Meaning rejoice when that person receives a blessing and you didn't. Able to take criticism. Recognizing who has authority over you. Slow to anger or to have your way, when you know you are right. Not always having to be the center of attention. Learning to listen to others when they need to vent. Enabling you to know how to pray for them.

Start your thinking process from the top!

May 6

2 Corinthians 5:7

"We walk by faith, not by sight."

Don't work failure into your plans by saying things like, "If my marriage fails I'll get a divorce. If my business fails I can always file bankruptcy."

If God doesn't hear me, I have insurance.

No general ever goes into battle planning to lose. What do you see at the inception of your dreams?

Shut the door, keep out the devil.

Gaze into the Kingdom of God and plan to win.

Line your pockets with, "In God We Trust!"

May 7

Hosea 4:6

*"My people are destroyed
for the lack of knowledge:
because thou has rejected knowledge,
I will also reject him."*

Lack of knowledge is not the same as unavailability. Knowledge may surround us but unless we apply it to our lives in making decisions it's useless.

We can't make excuses to God by saying "I didn't know" We live in an info explosion. Teachers, books, CDs TV, radio and internet provide us with all kinds of ways to stretch and increase our horizons by His WORD!

There is no reason to stay '**Dumb-in the-Box.**'

May 8

Matthew 16:18

"You are Peter and on this rock I will build my Church and the gates of hell will not prevail."

Jesus renamed Simon which meant unable and shaky, a leaf blowing in the wind to Peter. He changed his mind constantly.

How you feel or what others say about you is unimportant. You are who God says you are. He sees in you more than you can ever imagine.

Your potential is limited only by God, not others. Jesus chipped away at Simon until finally at Pentecost Simon was revealed as Peter meaning Rock. Rock also means the Truth.

May 9

Psalms 42:2

"My soul thirst for God, for the living God: when shall I come and appear before God."

If you want to grow in the Lord, it is important that you stay thirsty – never satisfied with what you know.

Jesus promises in **Matthew 5:6**, "Blessed are they which do hunger and thirst after righteousness for they shall be filled."

There are great benefits from getting to know your God. In His presence there is fullness of joy, because He hears and notices those who seek His face.

So DRINK!

May 10

Romans 12:2

"Be not conformed to this world; be transformed by the renewing of your mind."

Good morning believer. Do you know where your mind's at? Your soul is saved but your mind has to transform.

Stop believing every evil report. Don't try to get even. You are better because of the Blood. Stop letting your flesh dictate and allow your renewed spirit to be the shot caller. While others loose their minds, you focus on the Truth (Word of God).

This morning, check what your mind's is up to and make the proper adjustments.

May 11

Revelation 3:8

*"See, I have set before you an open door
and no one can shut it."*

Behind you a door has shut. The Lord has closed
it. You know you can't go back. In front of you a
new door has opened holding opportunities,
challenges, ministry, influence and a whole new
future.

The door to the past is sealed shut but the door to
the future has not opened yet. There's indication
it will. This is called the TRANSITION ZONE.
Now what?

Trust, Wait and Know He brought you out to
bring you in.

May 12

Isaiah 30:15

"In quietness and confidence shall be your strength."

It is God's gift of peace given right in the midst of labor and activity. Quietness is not the absence of problems. It is an undisturbed calm that says in the midst of tribulation, "Its ok. God is in control. He's got this."

Such calmness produces confidence.

Confidence = Assurance and Boldness.

Armed with these two potent spiritual forces, you move with new strength, determination and power.

May 13

Isaiah 11:3

"And shall make him of quick understanding in the fear of the Lord."

Quick understanding is a Hebrew expression meaning quick scented or detect by breath. The ability to detect and judge by the way something smells.

Children of God should be able to instantly discern what's behind every activity he comes in contact with, by learning to quickly surrender to the Lord.

Cling to Him like glue.

Can you smell what God is cooking right now?

May 14

Leviticus 19:31

"Regard not them that have familiar spirits, neither seek after wizards to be defiled by them. I am the LORD your God."

This subject keeps coming up, so let us deal with it.

A familiar spirit aids fortune tellers, witches, wizards. They give information about the person they are dealing with. They are coming into our churches masquerading as Pastors and Prophets. Before you let them lay hands on you, be led by the Holy Spirit or judge their fruit.

Leviticus 20:6 says "the soul that goes after them which have familiar spirits and go whoring after them, I will set my face against that soul and cut him off from among his people."

May 15

Romans 8:5

*"For they that are after the flesh
do mind the things of the flesh;
but they that are after the Spirit
the things of the Spirit."*

The Holy Spirit vs. Familiar spirits. Note Spirit
and spirits. He's God all by Himself.

Check out the vessel being used. What kind of
fruit does it bear? Does it elevate self or point
you to God at all times? Both spirits may comfort
you. But is it by the Word of God? The dead can
not speak to you, it's a spirit/demon that is
familiar with your past and present.

The Holy Spirits gets the future right every time.

May 16

Philippians 4:13

"I can do all things through Christ which strengthens me."

The next few days will be about the power of your tongue. Those that say they can and the ones who say they can't, are both right.

Words are the most powerful things in the universe. The words you speak has power to manifest themselves. They can free you or keep you in bondage.

I speak understanding into your lives today.

May 17

Genesis 1:1

"God created the heavens and earth."

We know God spoke worlds into existence. We know we are made in His image having the same ability to speak things into existence.

So we need to be careful not to pray the problem but instead, pray the solution. Not "Lord it's still here and getting worse."

We have used our tongue to pray defeat instead of "I believe I have received what I prayed for. I have confidence in your ability and wisdom for the best."

Even prayer produces after its own kind. The words God spoke creating the world, still stand today in obedience.

May 18

James 3:10

*"Out of the same mouth proceeds
blessing and cursing.
My brethren these things ought not be."*

Why do we speak negativity so easily, yet saying
something positive takes mental focus?

It's because we are born in sin. Negativity comes
easy even though we are a new creature.

Can Jesus hang with you all day or would you
have to watch your mouth?

Let's keep it real. When speaking about
ourselves and others, out of the mouth the heart
speaks.

May 19

Luke 1:20

"You shall be dumb not able to speak til the day these things are performed, because you didn't believe my words that will be done."

Zacharias and Elizabeth prayed for a child. Gabriel appeared to him saying God heard them. But he started to question. So Gabriel closed his mouth. He was unable to speak until later, when he agreed with God.

He had to be shut-down, because his words carried weight.

If we can't speak in faith, we need to shut our own mouths.

May 20

Psalms 24:7

"Lift up your heads O ye gates, everlasting doors."

Young people, new things introduced into society gets perverted some way.

Rap music for instance began fun entertainment, then became dark and foul. Hell understands the power of words which it speaks at supernatural speed into your spirits.

Backwards keeps you enslaved. Watch what's preached into your gates and doors. They are gateways into your spirits.

May 21

Isaiah 46:4

"Even to your old age "I am He; and even to grey hairs will I carry you; I have made, and I will bear; even I will carry and will deliver you."

Seniors this verse says that God won't change on you as you age and gray. You are still His child. He still hears you.

Note to the young. Many have more ailments than you. Asthmatic, high blood pressure, limping, stiff, coughing, knots and depressed.

Do not let anybody speak old on you. Speak health to your mind and body.

May 22

Joshua 24:15

*"As for me and my house,
we will serve the Lord."*

Men of God, take your stand without fear and lead by example.

Speak over the lives of your family members in prayer. Let your wives and kids know you have a made-up mind. Trust and believe they will be influenced.

Single men before you choose a wife and start a family, make sure God has first priority in her life.

Proverbs 18:22 says, He who finds a wife finds a good thing and obtains favor of the Lord, meaning He will bless that union.

May 23

Proverbs 12:18

"The tongue of the wise is health."

Some of us experienced healings from the last series on health. Some are still struggling with same health issues.

First remember God wants you healed and He gets no glory in your illness. So today speak to that thing in the name of Jesus everyday until there is no doubt. Let it know you know it does not belong to you.

Lay hands on it. Speak the Truth to it. Say by His stripes I am healed.

May 24

Exodus 23:25

"Ye shall serve the LORD your God, and he shall bless thy bread and thy water; and I will take sickness away from the midst of thee."

He also promises healing. Even while taking meds thank him for your healing,

While bathing or showering, lay hands on that area saying "Lord you are the God that heals me". Promise to serve Him with all your might and heart.

This body was not meant to last forever but to live on earth as it is in heaven – in divine health.

May 25

Mark 11:23

*"Whoever says to this mountain "be removed…
and does not doubt in his heart but believes
those things he says will be done, he will have
those things he says will be done, he will have
whatever he say."*

This concludes: Power of your tongue.

When reborn, healing became your birthright. We dealt with this particular mountain because money or anything else is secondary to your health.

Might take time, but even in pain SPEAK! This requires courage. Step into the circle with some soldiers. Agree and BELIEVE in what you say.

May 26

Isaiah 26:3

"I will keep him in perfect peace whose mind is stayed on me because he trust me."

CHECK UP TIME:

Do you know what your mind is up to? Is it on that person who hurt you? Maybe it's dwelling in anger or worrying about job security.

Could it be tripping off to *Guffy Land* by way of drugs? Wherever it is, fix what you can. Everything else give it to God and let Him figure it out.

Choose to bring your mind under subjection. This the perfect time to talk with Him honestly. He knows anyway and waits on you!

May 27

Genesis 3:11

"Who told you that you were naked?"

Who told you that your race is ugly? Who told you that you are a loser? Who said you are too old, too young?

Advertisers and Politician know this biblical principle, "that faith comes by hearing" and if you hear something often enough you will believe it. They know the masses will not check facts.

Advertisers use it to sell. Politicians use it to control. God uses it so you may have abundant life. Check out how God feels about you. He gave His very best for you – Himself. All he wants from you is YOU!

No one can make your feel inferior without your permission!

May 28

Proverbs 1:7

*"The fear of the Lord
is the beginning of knowledge;
but fools despise wisdom and instruction."*

Some people don't know nothing and don't wanna know nothing (Spirit of Dumb). Seekers make them nervous. The WORD calls them fools. What is the fear of the Lord? Proverbs 8:13 says fear anything the Lord hates. But we never know which ones will awake out their stupor and escape towards the Light.

We are to lift them up in prayer regardless. Someone did for us.

The fear of the Lord means the fear of being without Him in our lives.

Thank you so much Jesus!

May 29

I Thessalonians 4:16

*"The Lord himself will descend from heaven
with a shout with the voice of the archangel and
with the trumpet of God:
the dead in Christ will rise first:
Then we which are alive and remain will be
caught up together with them in the clouds
to meet the Lord in the air."*

Noah preached for 120 years and no one listened except his family.

Who will be the last to answer the Call? It could be your family member. No one knows the day nor the hour. Time is so close; He could come as you are reading this message.

Seriously Saints pay attention!

May 30

I Corinthians 10:31

"Whatsoever ye do, do all to the glory of God."

When trying to get closer to God, careful you are not inadvertently doing so from the flesh. How? By trying to move in your own strength. Unknowingly moving away from Him. A temptation to pat yourself on the back.

Remember when you are weak, He is strong. Through His mercy however, He will give you nudges to let you know something is not quite right. You might be in danger of getting self righteous, rather than glorifying God.

Know He wants you victorious at ALL times.

May 31

I John 5:4

"Everyone born of God overcomes the world."

When God tells you to dominate everything, He's speaking to the potential within you. This includes every habit because God clearly stated you can.

Some of you have resolved you are hooked forever. This is a lie, spoken by the Loser. It's not that you can't - it's that you won't. God will never demand you to do what He has not provided for.

So put down the candy, cigarettes and crack. The truth is you CAN!

Thoughts

June 1

Jeremiah 29:11

"For I know the thoughts that I think toward you, says the Lord, thoughts of peace not of evil to give you an expected end."

LIFE HAPPENS.

You can call off sick but who calls off dead? No matter where you go, life will find you.

Whether God gives you a command or promise at the beginning, at your expected end you need faith in the middle.

This is where you find peace. This is where you please God – in the middle. Now watch Him move!

June 2

Ephesians 6:14

"Stand therefore having your loins girt about with truth."

The Truth is, He loves you more than you can comprehend. In order for the armor to be effective, you must protect your reproductive area with the Truth.

Truth is a spiritual contraceptive, aborting Satanic lies in your spirit, allowing your true potential to be birthed.

Birth the Truth of God today. Meditate on its Power. Rejoice because He lives in YOU!

June 3

Philippians 3:14

"I press toward the mark for the prize of the high calling."

When delivered from Egypt, the Israelites said it was better there, because they missed the food. They grew tired of manna and sat around complaining about God's cooking. Lot's wife was warned not to look back. She did and was turned into a pillar of salt.

Sometimes when God is delivering us, he has to take us elsewhere.

Change can be scary. Let Him move you. Know because you are safe, it's all good. Just REST and Trust, He knows exactly where He's taking you!

June 4

Matthew 6:13

*"For Thine is the Kingdom
and the power and glory."*

Can't say our Father and not try to act like His
child.

Can't say who art in heaven, if not laying up
treasure there.

Can't say thy will be done, if I'm disobedient to
His Word

Can't say on earth as it is in Heaven, if I won't
serve Him HERE and NOW.

Can't claim His power, if I fear what men will do
to me.

Can't ask for daily bread and only eat His
WORD sometimes – Author Unknown

June 5

Psalms 139:24

"See if there is any wicked way in me"

Seems man will explore everything but himself. But David asks the Lord to check him over to see if he is spiritually healthy. He risked the pain and embarrassment of being found guilty of hidden and presumptuous sins.

It is possible to approach God with clean hands and a pure heart, but it takes honesty and commitment to the truth about ourselves, the flashlight that will not allow us to hide things in the heart that displeases our God.

June 6

Ephesians 5:19

"Speaking to yourselves in palms and hymns and spiritual songs, singing and making melody in your heart to the Lord."

God rides on sound. The sound of NOW. He created by sound. Action follows sound.

Your words create atmosphere. In the atmosphere of praise and worship, depression cannot occupy the same space. Anger cannot stay, fear has to vacate the premises. Even in worshipping Him, He protects you with love.

It's to our benefit to offer up songs to Him.

Hallelujah!! Let's go for a ride.

June 7

Romans 1:28

"They didn't like to retain God in their knowledge, God gave them over to a reprobate mind."

New Saints often ask if they have committed the unpardonable sin. If you are concerned, then you haven't.

The sin is not accepting Christ the sacrificial Lamb. He cannot forgive or pardon unrepentance. He will let you go on believing stupid stuff, like the Big Bang Theory.

It takes great faith to believe in explosions that result in perfect order.

God's life in you is what's explosive!

June 8

Numbers 33:55

"If you don't drive out the native population, everyone you let stay will become pricks in your eyes and thorns in your sides and shall vex you in the where you dwell."

Is God trying to move you higher or begin a ministry? What's stopping you? It may be unforgiveness, choice of entertainment, what others say you can or cannot do. What does God say?

Determine today to kill them from your heart and mind today!

June 9

Exodus 33:14

*"My presence will go with you
and I will give you rest."*

Rest is the ability to function at full capacity and strength during trials and tribulations. Jesus is our role model.

He was never caught off guard or taken by surprise. Even when trick questions were thrown at him, He handled His opponents with ease. He threw them off instead. Inner peace kept Him cool even in the face of opposition.

He promises to you this same peace and rest. Have a restful and peaceful day.

June 10

Psalms 121:1

*"I will lift up my eyes to the hills
from which comes my help."*

Something is happening in the Body of Christ. A shaking and shifting. We are being forced to rely on God as never before.

Things we relied on and got comfortable with in the past are being removed. Such as job security, relationships finances, etc.

God already knows how you will react, but you need to know the strength of your own faith in order to grow.

Look Up and seek first the Kingdom of Heaven. Victory is yours!

June 11

THE CENTER:

There are 594 chapters before Psalms 118 and 594 chapters after. Psalms 118 is the center of the Bible.

Actually, 118:8 is the very center which says, "**It is better to trust in the Lord than put your confidence in man.**"

Reflecting on past mistakes and disappointments ask yourself, what was the core? Peer pressure, enticed into drugs, abusing your body and other self-destructive behaviors?

They probably all have faces on them. Seek His Face instead.

You will not go wrong trusting God, the center of your joy!

June 12

John 15:16

"You have not chosen me but I have chosen you."

Jesus is the offspring of God and man. Scripture says He is the Word. WORD = the thought and intent of God. He always had Jesus in His mind and intentions. In other words, from a place of no space or time, He knew you were unable to save yourself. You would need help and mercy.

You were on His heart. He thought of you all the time. He is preoccupied with you all the time.

Thinking of Him more and more lately?

Look out - you might be falling in love!☺

June 13

Genesis 3:24

*"He placed at the east end
of the garden Cherubim."*

Cherubim are a high order of angels who protect the presence of God. The Holy Spirit is also called the Presence of God.

Ponder this. You in which the Holy Spirit dwells aka the Presence of God. Does God need protection? Of course not, but the meeting place does.

When seeking him out you need to enter in without distraction or sin. Wow! Alone in His PRESENCE. You are the meeting place.

Your job is to guard this Holy place as well!

June 14

Romans 8:8

"Those of the flesh can't please God."

Satan can no longer communicate with God because his spirit is dead. No wonder he is so preoccupied with death and those who fellowship with him.

He has no blood to offer. Faith does him no good. He always knew the Truth. So he felt once he planted the seed of doubt in mankind, its spirit would die, but he never counted on it to be born again.

The fact that God has entered the building causes the dead to Rise and Awake!

June 15

Isaiah 37:33-34

"He shall not come into this city
nor shoot an arrow there... by the way he came,
by the same way shall he return."

The Lord is speaking through the prophet Isaiah, telling Israel their enemy is coming but he will not be able to shoot even one arrow into their city.

We can have that same confidence. Our minds so saturated with the Word of God, our hearts so filled with His Spirit, that the enemy will have to flee the same way he came against us. By words. The words of God.

Remember Jesus in the wilderness?

June 16

Psalms 119:165

"Great peace have those who love your law, and nothing causes them to stumble."

In the path of every believer are booby traps, land mines and obstacles.

Satan's strategy is to keep you from reaching your destination. This great peace promised to those who love and trust the Lord is so profound that with it in our hearts we can be assured of passing safely through all danger zones that lie between you and your ultimate destination.

Nothing will cause you to stumble. God has put you in a win, win situation in this life as well as the next.

June 17

John 20:22

"He breathed on them and said to them receive the Holy Ghost."

It is God's nature to give and when he gives, He gives His very best (Himself). After all He gave His only begotten Son.

What is His motive? It is LOVE. All He asks is that you RECEIVE/ACCEPT what the name of Jesus affirms:

> *Let me save you.*
> *Just let me bless you.*
> *Let me live my life in you.*

He is able. He is waiting to Exhale.

All you need to do is INHALE and RECEIVE!

June 18

Isaiah 45:7

"I form the light and create darkness. I make peace and create evil.
I the Lord do all these things:"

Hold up! God creates darkness and evil? God deals with rebellion by removing Himself and letting the wicked and their children go into captivity which causes absence of Light. He says you do Boo!

Sin has its own built-in laws that takes care of itself. Like a seed it reproduces and bears its own fruit.

Need answers? The world says follow the money. God says follow ME!

June 19

Genesis 18:17

"The Lord said, Shall I hide from Abraham that thing which I do?"

Christians are not religious but relational. Friend of the Lord of Host, King of kings, Ancient of Days. He makes Hollywood's VIP list look like a grocery list. Talk about down to earth. You are on a first name basis with the Creator of Spirits.

Instead of magnificent titles, He said just call me Jesus. No other name given to man. Like Abraham, He calls you friend when you believe in him.

June 20

Jeremiah 33:3

*"Call to me and I will answer you and show you
great and mighty things
which thou knowest not."*

MIGHTY THINGS:

These mighty things are revelations of not only
who God is, but who you are as well. You know
God is the greatest, most awesome thing you will
encounter. After that is the revelation of who you
are.

This verse also refer to His name. Someone's
character. When you hear their name you have
certain expectations and images, good/bad. When
you hear the name of God what comes to mind?
Upon others hearing yours, what comes to mind
beloved?

June 21

Psalms 27:10

"When my father and mother forsake me, the Lord will take care of me."

Forsake means complete desertion, absolute rejection, total abandonment.

Even if your parents totally reject and desert you, you can still make it. As hurtful as parental neglect is, it does not mean the end. Even if good parents wanted to provide for you, but were unable to, your heavenly Father will provide or make it up to you later.

Draw strength from these experiences and move on. Vow to be a better parent and let it go!

June 22

John 10:27

"My sheep hear my voice."

What's your mind listening to now? To hear God, you must also recognize the sound of the Deceiver. He is always trying to pop in his CD, entitled "LOSER" to play in your head. Tracks like "All by Myself" or "Go Ahead, No One Will Ever Know but You" or "Did God Really Say?"

Sing a different song or change the lyrics from "I'll Never Win" to "Too Legit to Quit" or "I Kissed a Girl and I Liked it" to "I Read the Word and I Loved It, Transformed My Mind and Made Me New".

June 23

Matthew 16:19

"I will give to you the KEYS of the Kingdom of Heaven; and whatever you BIND on earth will be bound in heaven; whatever you loose on earth shall be loosed in heaven."

Keys are revelations or understanding the 'word of 'God. Bind meant to Declare or state officially. Open your mouth – declare!

There is a declaration in heaven waiting on you because you are speaking able to manifest things from heaven or hell. Agree with Heaven.

Speaking and praying new revelation in your life to whomever is reading this today!

June 24

James 1:22

"Be ye doers of the word and not hearers only, deceiving your own selves."

Knowing something does not mean you are doing something.

If you don't change something today your tomorrow will not change. Habits tell your future. What you repeat is who you are. Know your Father has not called you to mediocrity/average. You are set apart to do great things Child of God. Remove the handcuffs off Him and allow Him to expand your boarders.

Let us put His Word in Practice.

June 25

Ephesians 6:18

"Praying always with prayer and supplication in the Spirit and watching thereunto with all perseverance and supplication for all saints."

Brothers and Sisters our families are being beheaded, babies sliced in half, young girls kidnapped for prostitution and crucified. Except for the babies, they refused to compromise their faith.

Please keep our fellow Christians in your prayers daily. We need each other. We never know when we will need to call upon the saints of God on our behalf.

June 26

Psalms 138:8

"The Lord will perfect that which concerns me."

Every area of our lives is in a state of development and a learning process. We are growing by His divine time table with a design to it. Despite how it looks, we are making progress.

As our faith grows, understanding of His purpose and ours is expanding. Our priorities are changing as we learn what's really important.

Know God is perfecting and completing you. He loves you too much to leave you the way you are.

June 27

Isaiah 54:14

"In righteousness you shall be established thou shall be far from oppression, for thou shall not fear; and from terror; for it shall not come near thee."

We can literally dismiss from our thinking any oppressive thoughts, replacing them with positive affirmations and images.

Whenever any wrong thoughts come to your mind, you need to VERBALLY speak a word of refusal to them. Say, "I do not accept that thought. Return to where you came from, I know it's not my Jesus because He does not think that way." I have the mind of Christ.

Do this and oppression will have to leave you alone.

June 28

Jeremiah 31:16-17

"They shall come back from the land of the enemy... your children shall come back to their own border."

When the ark was done, God said to Noah, "Come into the ark" you and your household" This word applies today. A flood of tribulations and persecution is coming.

Get your family together and bring them in. One feature of the last day move of the Spirit is family salvation and unity. Your children will return before final darkness on earth. We have much to do.

Believe and be ENCOURAGED!

June 29

Proverbs 26:11

*"As a dog returns to his vomit,
so a FOOL returns to his folly."*

We know nothing is too hard for our God, not even YOU. Be careful not to return to old habits and friends out of boredom or loneliness. They mean you no good.

Some of you are destined for ministry, so bust out of 'Dumb-in-the-Box' and keep stepping.

Your Father's plans are to move you forward; beyond anything you could imagine as the HEAD Not the tail. A Lender not a Borrower and that's just the beginning. How soon is up to you.

Holy POTENTIAL!

June 30

Matthew 10:34-39

"I did not come to bring peace but a sword, I have come to turn a man against his father, a daughter against her mother, a daughter-in-law against her mother-in-law; a man's enemies will be the member of his own household."

Do not fret when family members shun you because you are a believer. They weren't feeling Jesus either. In his own town He could not perform miracles there.

Stand, be encouraged and pray. Their salvation has been promised to you.

Thoughts

Reveal

July 1

John 11:33

"Jesus therefore when he saw her weeping, and the Jews who were weeping with her, groaned in spirit, and troubled himself."

Jesus wept as a human, but raised Lazarus from the dead as God. As the divine Son of God, he knew Lazarus would be sick and die and brought to life.

Know that he is willing to trouble himself for you. Trust him to respond to some dead issues for your sakes while other things need to die.

He will raise the dead ones by divine intervention.

July 2

Galatians 1:10

"Do I now persuade men or God?"

INFLUENCE is a wonderful gift. With influence you need not run after money, your needs are met (seek ye first the kingdom and all these things will be added to you). You influence others to Christ as he quietly manifests in your life.

We persuade God by faith and obedience. God and the devil use influence to save or damn souls. Both need your permission. This is the only way they are equal.

Before you act, check out directions. In checking, if persuaded by the TRUTH, mysteries are revealed. Do the math! Where do lies get you? Tripping and falling in the dark.

July 3

Romans 8:28

"All things work together for good to them that love God to them who are the called according to his purpose."

This Word is easy when there are no storms, but the hardest things to bear have, in reality, been best for us. It either drives us from God or brings us nearer to Him.

The guilt of Judas drove him to suicide. However, Peter was transformed from denying Jesus, into the Rock.

Look on times of sorrow and trouble as turning points in your life Child of God.

July 4

Romans 8:19

*"Earnest expectation of the creature waits for
the manifestation of the sons of God."*

BEING:

You were created to BE. God is the Supreme
Being. You are the human being. So be who you
are. He'll alert you of needed adjustments. Make
self examinations, then if all is well, continue on
with caution.

It's easy to get sucked into others perception of
you. You will disappoint your self and others are
let down as well. They need you to be who God
created you to BE.

Earth is searching for REAL. Until He moves
you, grow where you are planted. He will use
you THERE.

July 5

Ephesians 2:10

"For we are His workmanship"

You are walking down a dark street on your way home, when you notice ten young men walking behind you. Which scenario would you prefer: They are coming from a gang, a bar meeting or Bible study?

Even atheist if honest would answer bible study. Where God's people are, there is light.

Workmanship in original Greek means poetry. As people observe you, they can see and hear the work of God. Christians are God's artistic expression.

Our hearts vibrate in syncopation with the heart of our Father.

July 6

I Corinthians 4:1

"Let us be looked upon as ministers of Christ and Steward of the mysteries of God."

Watchers of His mysteries. What an honor! How do we guard these mysteries? By studying and correcting error. Alerting others of false prophets. Able to explain why you believe.

So sure, that even if an angel of light appeared to you, you would know instantly if he were speaking the truth.

You are privileged Child of God. Be safe and pray for your country today.

July 7

Psalms 91:4

"He shall cover thee with His feathers and under His wings shalt thy trust."

The Eagle:

When the mother feels the baby birds are old enough, she begins putting things in the nest to make them uncomfortable. Eventually, they will jump or be kicked out, but the father watches carefully and catches them if they fall. This process is repeated until they learn how to fly and soar.

God is willing to be misunderstood in order for you to mature. He won't let you be tempted beyond your ability.

July 8

James 4:8

*"Draw nigh to God
and He will draw nigh to you."*

The eagle has two sets of eye lids. When he is being chased by his enemy, he flies towards the sun where they can't follow him.

God has given us two sets of eyes as well, natural and spiritual. You don't walk by sight but by faith. His main enemy to his babies is the snake. When he finds it, he takes it miles high and crashes it against a rock.

The first liar appeared to man as a serpent, but he is crushed beneath our feet on the **Rock** – Jesus.

July 9

Isaiah 40:31

"They that wait on the Lord shall renew their strength."

Many are experiencing spiritual dullness and struggling with their faith.

The molting process can cause depression and make this powerful bird very weak. At one time he could see its prey a mile high, but he loses his vision, unable to hunt. It loses its desire to eat.

The beak becomes so encrusted with calcium he's unable to lift its head.

Been there?

July 10

Isaiah 40:31

"They that WAIT on the Lord shall renew their strength."

This Word encourages us to Wait. God uses the eagle because of its strength and wisdom. But most important the molting process he must go through.

He gets weak, loses his feathers and sheds skin. He can't fly in this condition. His partner is a life partner and usually they go through together.

He lives about 70 years. Molting usually takes place around the age of 30. This Process can cause and make this majestic bird to walk like a turkey.

Know this thing will not be forever.

To be cont'd...

July 11

Isaiah 40:31

"They that WAIT on the Lord shall renew their strength."

During this molting process they pull out their oily dirty feathers. They will turn on other molting eagles. Not all make it.

Some just give up becoming discouraged and suicidal. They gather together in one place and choose some area of a mountain where the sun can shine directly on them, while waiting to live or die.

While sun bathing other older eagles who have gone through the same process, begin screaming loudly and dropping meat overhead for nourishment.

To be cont'd

July 12

Psalms 103:5

"That thy youth is renewed like the eagle."

The ones who decide to fight, upon hearing their elders and intercessors screaming encouragement to eat, will bang their beaks and scratch their nails down to nothing, sensing new ones will grow in.

When complete, the eagle will become genetically very young. It will stretch forth its wings and soar off for many years to come.

For a Christian the molting process can take place anytime in life. Don't be so quick to discount your elders nor coming together in worship. There is an anointing when gathering on one accord. You must eat the Word for strength. The stronger the wind the higher you will fly.

July 13

Romans 16:20

"The God of Peace will crush Satan under your feet shortly."

You have been ASSURED the victory and what your God has planned for you is so huge, your enemy will be sorry he ever bothered you. Your deliverance is going to be such an embarrassment to the enemy that he will never try the same tactic again to oppose you.

If it seems you are not getting any feedback from heaven, know the Teacher is always silent during the test. You hush and be still as well.

Zip It!

July 14

Luke 10:17

"Devils are subject to us in your name."

At times we need to be reminded that God and Satan are not equal. However, they both have to get our permission to get involved in our lives.

God seems to be winning some days. Other days seems like Satan has the upper hand and we are stuck in the middle with no say.

Spiritual authority is not a tug of war. The devil is defeated but he can deceive us into thinking he has more authority than us. You have authority over the Kingdom of darkness. He hopes you just don't get it.

I declare we DO!

July 15

Romans 8:28

"We know in all things God works for the good of those who love him, who have been called according to his purpose."

God will allow you to be outside of things for His purpose. You might find yourself doing things to get others to change opinions about you because you feel shutout.

When you understand God has done this, your view of being shut out will be from a higher perspective.

There is no limit outside. He will take you out for revelation and clarity.

Speak Lord! Stir up gifts!

July 16

I Corinthians 14:33

"God is not the author of confusion."

Ever tried sharing Christ with someone or a particular truth in the Bible only to have them jump totally to another subject or scripture.

This a trick of the adversary. Gently, point this out to them and ask, "Could we please stay focused? We can discuss this next or at another time." Maybe even explain to them, if you feel led, this is exactly what the enemy desires. If they insist on continuing in this way, know God does not deal in confusion.

Abort, pray and move on.

Know your enemy.

July 17

Matthew 21:19

"Let no fruit grow in you ever again and immediately the fig tree withered away."

Its roots were taking up valuable nutrients out of the soil. Branches soaked up sun, leaves drank in the rain. Taking and giving nothing.

Fear, poverty, illness, anything negative whether it be people, places or things that take up valuable space or energy producing no positive results, can be rooted out and cursed from your life.

He has promised to prune, anything that hinders your growth.

July 18

Proverbs 18:21

"Death and life are in the power of the tongue."

Are you believing God for something? Beware of the enemy saying in your head after a bad thought. "See you really don't believe. You're weak and will never receive it". As long as you believe with your heart and speak with your mouth, you are not doubting. You don't have to accept that lie.

The EVIDENCE of things not seen means proof is coming! Impossibility is God's specialty.

So BELIEVE and SPEAK His Word over and over again. Say "By His stripes I am HEALED.

Don't retreat – RELOAD!

July 19

Luke 11:1-9

"Don't bother me...
The door's locked; my children are all down
for the night; I can't get up to give anything."

Jesus uses this parable in response to his disciples' request, "Master teach us how to pray". A friend needs bread for an unexpected guest. The friend finally gave in because he was persistent.

Jesus ends with knock and it will be opened to you. He is encouraging you to stand your ground. Don't ask once but continue. Because you ask more than once does not mean you have no faith.

July 20

Psalms 119:114

"Thou art my hiding place."

When your heart is open to new possibilities, you are no longer a victim of circumstances, because you know your steps are ordered by the Lord. You understand you have options and your mentality changes.

As you sense the presence of God, you will operate from this secret place. A place of peace and creativity. Anger or fear can not follow you there. You are in a win, win situation.

Your mission today should you wish to take it is find this HIDING PLACE!

July 21

Psalms 110:3

*"Your people shall be volunteers
in the day of your power."*

Do not give up on loved ones who seem indifferent now. Many of them will be the first to volunteer when the Lord pours out His Spirit on the earth and go forth in the last days against hell.

This army will be tremendous and relentless, because they know and understand their God. They will be even more grateful for forgiveness they have received.

Continue to pray for them. It is the driest land that responds to moisture and rain.

July 22

Psalms 73:17

"Then I understood their end."

David asks why sinners seem to prosper while the righteous attending church are tested. He wonders if he's on the wrong team.

As he entered the sanctuary he realized the church is the link between this world and the next. Truth is proclaimed there. It is an empowerment station. It is group worship, supernatural healing for the mind and body.

We learn this is not a fairy tale, but truly has a happy ending for which the wicked haven't a clue.

July 23

Psalms 115:5

"eyes have they but they see not."

The U.S. Military use's night equipment, enabling them to see their enemy at night. One is attached to a scope enabling them to see both with natural eye sight and the other with enhanced night vision.

Because you are a soldier of God you have the capability of seeing with your natural eye and in the spirit. You will experience dark times, but you are armed with the Spirit of Truth and will be able to see and react to the enemy accordingly.

July 24

Hebrews 11:1

"Faith is the substance of things hoped for."

Has Satan stolen your hope? The Word says we cannot please God without faith. Without hope we have no faith because our hope has no substance.

Check to see where the enemy has stolen hope from you. Then claim it back. Know your faith will heal you and others, save souls, fix finances and cast out demons. Reclaiming your hope can impact the world.

The Loser has come to steal, kill and destroy. Take him out with the WORD!

July 25

Psalms 91:14-15

"Because he set his love upon me... He shall call upon me and I will answer him. I will be with him in trouble; I will deliver him."

Many had a rough couple of months. Sickness, stolen property, broken hearts, job disputes, marital problems, aging parents and death of loved ones.

These things are part of the human condition. Jesus knows how to give you peace in each and every one of these circumstances.

In your heart is a throne. Move over and let the Prince of Peace sit there!

July 26

Matthew 5:6

"Blessed are they that hunger and thirst."

There is a song called "FRESH" The singer is telling God that he's tired of doing the same thing, the same way every day. He wants to do something eyes haven't seen and ears haven't heard.

Yea I said! Then the sling shot theory came to mind. Sometimes you have to let God hold you back like a rock in a slingshot. The further you are pulled back, the further you will go.

When He lets you go, you are flung into your destiny with such force, that you break through barriers known and unknown.

Waiting is the key. Be prepared.

July 27

Galatians 6:9

***"Let us not be weary in well doing, in due
season we will reap if we faint not."***

In giving and serving, you may never receive
recognition or thank you. Those you try to help
may be the very ones who turn on you or won't
help if you are in need.

Learn early in the game your Father sees all. He
will reward your kindness and send another in
your path to bless you. The love of God will
flow freely through you.

Develop a Servant's Heart and He will delight
you in ways you thought impossible.

July 28

Psalms 8:4

*"What is man that thou art mindful of him
and care for him?"*

The universe is continually expanding at the speed of light. Yet its Creator loves you so much, He will bless those around you just because it makes you happy. He calls you friend. He will curse those who want to do you harm, while angels watch with curiosity.

We all ask "Who does that?" Hell is expanding also and people actually want to spend eternity there. The question is to do what?

July 29

Romans 12:2

"transformed by the renewing of your mind."

Time for a random mind check.

What is it up to? Is it just running around *Willy Nilly* without a leash? Mental cruise control does not work for a believer. Your mind must be brought under subjection to the obedience of Christ.

Someone trying to hold you back? Speak the TRUTH to that mountain.

Say God is my SOURCE. Then Watch!

July 30

Matthew 18:3

"Verily I say to you except ye be converted and become as little children ye shall not enter into the Kingdom of Heaven."

Some may say, "I tried and nothing happened" Look at the childish heart. If you tell a child you're taking him to Disneyland, that child does not say if we go, but continually and faithfully asks, "Are we there yet?"

This is NOW kind of faith. They see themselves THERE and won't let up because Daddy said so.

Jesus asks when I come will I see your faith? Can your Daddy see your faith?

Are you there yet?

July 31

Jesus described himself as the Bread, the Light, the Way, the Truth, Living Water, the Resurrection, the Door, the True Vine the Lamb of God and the ROCK.

The Truth Lights the Way through the Door to eternal Life. The Bread of Heaven and Living Water (His Word) feeds and sustains your journey through the wilderness. If you fall He is your Resurrection.

Trouble standing and your vision blocked by obstacles and Doubt? Stand on the **Rock** which lifts you higher to SEE over everything.

Thoughts

August 1

Luke 3:22

*"You are my beloved Son
in whom I am well pleased."*

Jesus was about to start ministry. His Father let him know he was pleased. He was confident when the Holy Spirit led him into the wilderness away from everyone to be tempted by Satan for 40 days.

Except for the last three, the Scripture is not clear as to all the temptations, but it must have been relentless.

It irritates Satan when you know you're in the will of God. Stay encouraged beloved and use this time wisely.

He won't bring you this far to leave you.

August 2

Leviticus 16:2

"I will appear in the cloud upon the mercy seat."

Appear means to see intellectually, perceive, to hear understand and learn, reveal self, position of trust. He said He would cause them to know and understand Him. The glory of God – the true nature of a thing.

This is really mercy because God doesn't have to show you anything. He promised you would see if you open your "eyes." You open your eyes, when you hunger and thirst for Him.

August 3

Matthew 6:26

"Behold the fowls of the air, for they sow not,
neither do they reap nor gather into barns;
yet your heavenly Father feeds them.
Are ye not much better than them."

Said the Robin to the Sparrow, "I would really like to know why these anxious human beings rush about and worry so."

Said the Sparrow to the Robin, "Friend, I think that it must be that they have no heavenly Father such as cares for you and me."

Somewhere over the rainbow, blue birds fly.
Birds fly over the rainbow,
why then oh why can't I?
If happy little blue birds fly beyond the rainbow,
why, oh why can't I?

August 4

Philippians 4:6-7

"Be careful for nothing but in everything by prayer and supplication with thanksgiving let your request be known to God and the peace of God which passes all understanding shall keep your hearts and minds through Christ Jesus."

He commands us to STOP worrying about ANYTHING, so it must be possible to obtain this supernatural state of mind. Peace you won't even comprehend neither the world.

Be glad you are not of this world Little One.

August 5

Luke 2:40

*"The child grew and became strong in the spirit,
filled with wisdom
and the grace of God was upon him."*

Grace is not only forgiveness of sins but empowerment. The Word says Jesus became strong in wisdom and grace was upon him.

Why did he need grace? Because he stripped himself of all divine privileges. Therefore, he needed grace's empowerment as a man to walk in wisdom on this earth.

If Jesus had to grow and learn, so do we.

August 6

Acts 27:23-24

*"There stood by me this night the angel of
God... Saying fear not Paul;
thou must be brought before Caesar.
To God has given thee all them
that sail with thee:"*

When the storm raged against the boat and its
crew, Paul made a choice, circumstances or
GOD. He has promises for every trial, test,
temptation and need.

Let us be Fearless and Relentless shouting, "I
BELIEVE God" to handle every obstacle and
trial.

AMEN!

August 7

I Timothy 5:16

*"If any man or woman that believes has widows
let them relieve them
and let not the church be charged that it may
relieve them that are widows."*

Even though it's not the Church's total responsibility, most times if you hear the word widow, it's about the woman who gave her last to shame believers and widows for not giving their last. However, God is concerned about her. We should be as well.

If you know one in need, bless her even if her church or family won't.

He will pay you back!

August 8

Warning! FMSM (Feed My Sheep Ministries) is not for the faint hearted. This next series is on the BLOOD of JESUS. I already know the enemy does not want this one to go forth. When I was text messaging this series on the BLOOD, it disappeared for no reason. As I was typing to put in book form, my computer deleted this part.

On that note: some will be offended by this topic, JWs Catholics, a couple Christians and Muslims, Blacks, Whites, Atheist, young and some Twilight fans.

If you decide to hang in there with a seeking mind, I promise you will be blessed on this powerful subject.

August 9

Exodus 12:13

"When I see the blood I will pass over you and the plague shall not be upon you to destroy you when I smite the land of Egypt."

The Blood = protection. God did not say He would bless Jews and curse Egyptians. They could have chosen God so that the Death Angel would have passed over them as well.

Prayer today is that those who chose to stay regarding this powerful topic and favor on them and their families.

August 10

Leviticus 17:11

"Life of the flesh is in the blood."

Why is God so concerned with blood? Hopefully this series will answer some questions for all of us and increase our faith with Holy boldness and help us to know who we are.

The blood is not life, but carries life. Life itself is spiritual but must have a physical carrier just as thoughts needs a physical brain. Human blood has the capacity to carry the life of God. As a believer your very DNA changes. Hereditary diseases have been known to disappear.

By faith you are a new Creature!

August 11

Romans 8:29

"That he might be the firstborn among many brethren."

We are all God's creation, but not all of are His children. The minute Mary accepted the Word that Gabriel brought to her, a baby was formed in her womb. You are a family member by faith in His Blood. Joint heir to his throne.

There may be something you need to agree with God on, so that thing can be birthed in you.

Like Mary, He will not force himself upon you. It has to be mutual consent.

Agree quickly!

August 12

Matthew 1:20

**"That which is conceived in her
is of the Holy Ghost."**

The female egg has no blood; neither does the
male sperm.   However, at conception the two
come together in the fallopian tube and new life
begins.

At this point the blood type is determined.
Afterward it is protected by the placenta from the
mother's blood into the fetus. When there is a
dispute as to the father of a child, there is a blood
test (baby and father).

Jesus was Son of God/son of man. Humanity and
Heaven came together here on earth.

August 13

Proverbs 6:16-19

"Six things the Lord hate, yes seven are an abomination to Him."

Unlike fixed tissues the blood is fluid and mobile. It's free to move through the body and supply fixed cells with nourishment and carry off waste products and ashes of waste products. This process is called metabolism.

This is what the blood of Jesus does. Each one of us is a cell in the Body of Christ. If there is an injury to the body the blood rushes to that injured part to repair and heal.

The Word says they will know us by the love we show to one another. God says to sow strife is an abomination. Instead of pray for healing of that other person. That the body of Christ is healthy.

August 14

I Corinthians 15:47, 49

"The first man is of the earth.
The second man is the Lord from heaven.
We have borne the image of the earthly.
We shall also bear the image of the heavenly."

Christ could partake of man's flesh but not his blood. Because he did not have one drop of Adam's blood meant it was sinless.

Our flesh is sinful because it is fed or nourished by sinful blood. Just like sin entered the blood stream spiritually, it is removed the same way.

August 15

Romans 6:7

"He that is dead is freed from sin."

Antitoxins and Antibodies build up after a while in the body. The same happens in the Believer.

Immunity from sin strengthens him. How? Through accepting the Blood and dying to self. Trusting its power to save and cover all his circumstances, he starts to develop a desire to please God.

There is an intimacy with this particular creation. What other creature did He express interest in living His holy life through?

Ponder this! This BLOOD'S for you.

August 16

John 19:30

"It is FINISHED."

What part of finished man did not understand? Finished meant he did not and could not offer any of his own works to pay for sin. So hell plays along with these deceptions which are a slap in the face of God.

Count the "Hail Mary's" on the rosary" then count the "Our Fathers" What's wrong with this picture? Did Mary have to shed blood? Didn't she have to receive the Holy Ghost just like the rest of us?

Black people did you know Mohammed called you Raisin Heads and believed God did not have a son? But where is he? Dead. Why do Mormons baptize the dead?

To be cont'd

August 17

John 19:30

"It is FINISHED."

What good is the blood if you can keep being reincarnated until you get it right? We are not saved by our own works but by His Grace. Ladies and Black folk, before joining or continuing a belief system, make sure to check its history. Are you included in the BLOOD covenant, is there one?

If a female Mormon is resurrected the man has to call you forth then go on to populate empty planets. Eternally pregnant? Oh joy! Muslims fair a little better. You are there for their sexual pleasure becoming virgins over and over again forever.

Is this about sex or the blood?

August 18

John 19:30

"IT IS FINISHED."

Jehovah Witnesses would like to make Jesus an angel, but the Blood covenant was between God and man. Besides angels have no blood. Saved!

Saved from what? Atheist and some other religions say there is no hell. Jesus shed blood to keep you from an eternity so horrible He could not bear it – so He bore it for you.

If there is no hell, then who needs the BLOOD? Beware of those who make mockery of the Blood of the Lamb.

Watch who you join forces with.

August 19

Leviticus 17:14

*"Ye shall not eat the Blood
of no manner of flesh."*

Jews drain all the blood from their meats. This is called *Kosher*. Where do you think Hollywood came up with the concept of vampires?

Basically they said, "Let's make fun of the Blood covenant by drinking it."

Oh Yeah! As long as they feed on human blood they'll gain eternal life. After all, it's only entertainment. Right?

Think about it Twilight fans. "Where do they want to go with this? Better yet, did they really think about it?"

August 20

Romans 12:2

*"Be ye transformed
by the renewing of your mind."*

This one will take a minute.

Black Folks! Why is it we fall prey to Jedi mind tricks?

The Nation of Islam was created by Wallie D. Fard. He told them that Christianity was a White man's religion. Ok but did anyone notice he himself was a White man?

How could this happen? This was all in their face. They were no longer interested in the Gospel or the Blood covenant. Thus they became blinded. Until this day they call him Master Fard Muhammad.

August 21

Jedi Mind Tricks:

Ellen White was a Seventh-Day Adventist prophetess. One of her teachings was Amalgamation which meant Black people were the offspring of man and beast.

Many Blacks still attend this "church". One individual says he knows for a fact, that behind closed doors some American SDAs believe her writings applies to the entire Black race.

Question? What animal have you ever seen after being shaved and the skin is Black?

Later in life, Ellen discovered she was part Black. I do believe God has a sense of humor.

Why does hell fight this race so much? Could fear be driving this bus?

August 22

Acts 10:34

"God is no respecter of persons."

Hell is no respecter of persons either. So why does it fear the Black race so much? Even though racism occurs all over the world, Christianity chose only the Black race to dehumanize. You never hear of Asian, White, Hispanics, etc. depicted as inhuman, only Blacks in the early church.

Note hell will only war against those it feels are a threat of some kind. Could it be the influence he has upon the world good or bad?

Scientist are now able to trace by DNA of the first woman, which was Eve. They found her to be Black. God said her seed would bruise the devil's head and he would bruise his head.

She was forgiven but there was no provision made for him. The Blood covenant began there. He has been warring against her and her children ever since with identity crisis. Know who you are Children of God.

August 23

Proverbs 6:15-19

"God hates strife among brethren. He says it is an abomination."

All believers are related by His BLOOD. Yet God made the Black race uniquely visual. Why would God allow this? The world hates him (the Black race), but will emulate him whenever possible.

If he ever gets the revelation of who he is, he's a danger to Hell and its followers. If he breaks through and stops believing lies about himself, revealing the glory of God, the whole human race will be blessed.

The gates of hell shall not prevail against the TRUTH and Blood of Jesus.

"We shall overcome"
              -Reverend Martin Luther King Junior.

August 24

Hosea 4:6

"My people are destroyed for the lack of knowledge because thou rejected knowledge I will also reject thee."

A couple of years ago the news reported the Vatican would baptize aliens if the opportunity presented itself. I thought that's odd.

So I did some research and found out the Vatican is using a telescope which is the most powerful in the world.

Even though they didn't name it, it is called the **Lucifer Project**.

They are looking and waiting on something.

Got Blood.

To be cont'd

August 25

Matthew 1:8

*"That which is conceived in her
is of the Holy Ghost."*

Why is the Vatican interested in aliens? They're waiting on The Messiah and say Mary was impregnated by an alien.

The devil either tries to deny the deity of Christ or focuses on Jews and Blacks to keep them out of the Blood covenant.

At any rate, it really doesn't matter if Jesus was blue or purple. It's about the Blood not the skin. Hell wants to keep division among the human race. When born again, your very DNA changes because you are a new creature. You are no longer bound by sin and you become open for miracles from heaven. You are no longer of this world (NOTW)

Question: If aliens exist, who created aliens?

August 26

John 14:6

"I am the WAY, the TRUTH and the LIFE: No man comes to the Father but by Me."

The enemy has tried to creep into the church various ways. Mostly through the ignorance of the Blood.

Avoid deception. Know the Blood covenant was not between angels, aliens or any other creation.

Beware of organizations that baptize the dead, that do not believe hell exists or where you can buy a candle and light it for the dead. Once again if that were the case why do we need the Blood?

Remember He is the only Way, the Truth and the Life.

August 27

Exodus 12:1-7

"On the 10th day of this month every man shall take for himself a lamb for a household."

Although each person must individually put his faith in Christ, we as parents and head of households can cover our homes and families under the protection of the BLOOD, creating an atmosphere of faith restricting the work of the enemy.

You can stand boldly before God and say "Dear God, I am interceding for my family." None of them will be lost even when visible evidence says different.

August 28

Matthew 13:44

"Kingdom of heaven is like a treasure."

There's priceless treasure in the Kingdom of God. However, God saw something in you. You were purchased at the highest price ever possible. Yet we live like we were brought in a yard sale.

What others saw as junk; God saw a precious treasure in you. The devil can counterfeit many things except the BLOOD of Jesus. He hates this message because he has absolutely no answer for it. It is DONE!

Got Blood?

August 29

II Timothy 2:3

"...endure hardness as a good solider..."

Because of the BLOOD, know its revelation can attract opposition. The enemy may try to scare or discourage you. So understand the nature of the conflict.

Good generals study the battlefield to get the lay of the land before sending troops to battle. We must do the same. We are at war. Satan is increasing his forces.

The battlefield is the hearts and minds of men.

August 30

John 15:13

"No greater love... than to lay down ones life for his friends."

If you are born again, you are a blood brother of Christ. You have in a sense taken your wrist and placed them against His bloody wrist and entered into a blood covenant with Him.

We are all related by the covenant with the same Father. If someone comes against me, we have sworn to protect each other. I regard your life, health, family, and finances as though they were mine. We have the same Father and enemy.

Today I will go to war for you in every way I know through the Blood and Power of Jesus Christ.

Amen!

August 31

II Corinthians 10:4

"The weapon of our warfare are not carnal but mighty in God for pulling down strong holds..."

Some of those weapons are the name of Jesus, Word of God and the Blood of the Lamb.

With such an arsenal we have blessed assurance. In pleading the Blood remember it is not a magic formula but by faith a spiritual principal.

Apply the Blood over your lives. This means you can apply a blood line around your, mind, business, school Apartment complex, etc.

Try and apply it.

Thoughts

September 1

John 1:29

*"Behold the Lamb of God
which takes away the sin of the world!"*

Note it says the **Sin**, not the sins.

The seven ways Jesus shed his Blood means it was perfect and complete. It is complete for women, Blacks, Jews, old and young.

Hope this series has provided understanding and knowledge you can work with.

Before joining anything, make sure they are not working their own way to heaven.

Amen!

September 2

John 14:12

"...anyone who believes in me will do the same works I have done and even greater works..."

Dare to dream and dare to dream Big. So big you will have to rely on God.

If we question God's ability, we insult His integrity and strength. We should be able to lay hands on the sick and they recover - cast out demons as Jesus did. We should start in our own homes.

When thinking and dreaming of unimportant things, override them with scripture. Expect and know He loves to start with NOTHING.

Let him use your passions to serve wherever possible.

September 3

II Corinthians 5:7

"We walk by faith not by sight."

Because God's people walk by faith and not what we see, this gives us power over our emotions. We will not find ourselves in jail because we could not handle rejection or shoot up the work place after being fired or contemplate suicide.

We understand God is our ultimate Source. He won't let us fall.

Continue to go by what He has said, "You are a blessed people, destined for victory through Him."

Walk in obedience knowing all Heaven has your back today.

September 4

II Chronicles 20:23-24

"After they finished slaughtering men from Seir they helped to destroy one another."

When others try to destroy you, Father says "I've got this" Stand Still. Go on praising Him. You won't have to lift a finger.

Observe as they get confused and turn or each other. Judah sent out the praise team before his army. Upon arrival all the enemies were dead. Your enemies don't even know they are dead. So let them lie and hate, because PRAISE is what you do.

God is with you always!

September 5

Genesis 1:26

*"God said, let us make man in our image,
in our likeness."*

All things are composed of whatever they came from and contain the potential of that particular source.

Plants only have the potential of that particular source. Plants only have the potential of its seed. An orange will not become a chicken.

God created you by speaking to Himself. You came out of God bearing His image and likeness. So who's your daddy?

Be a Blessing and dream Big for Him today.

Cling to Him!

September 6

Genesis 11:6

"The Lord said, if as one people speaking the same language they have begun to do this, then nothing they plan to do will be impossible for them."

God said, "If I don't interfere they will become able to do **anything** they think about and plan."

God did interfere in the building of the tower by confusing their language but He didn't stop them from thinking.

Anything you carry from thought to action is within your power to accomplish!

September 7

Isaiah 29:19

"The humble also shall increase their joy in the LORD"

Many Christians believe as the world, humility is soft spoken, weak and non-confrontational. True humility is absolute obedience and dependence on God. It puts Him first others second and ourselves third in all things.

Humility is not self-demeaning but living boldly empowered by God. A humble Child of God in reality, is a spiritual terrorist who fears nothing but God.

Meekness is power under control. May your joy increase today!

September 8

Matthew 10:32

*"Whomever therefore shall confess me
before men, him will I confess
also before my Father which is in heaven.
But whoever denies me before men,
him will I also deny before my Father."*

If people are surprised that you are a Christian, it's time to do a self examination.

A Believer on the down-low is not only missing out on intimacy with the Father but an opportunity to help others that need to know Him.

September 9

Isaiah 26:3

"I will keep him in perfect peace whose mind is stayed on Me because he trusts Me."

You may know someone or experiencing yourself mental illness.

When Christians dwell in a land they influence society. The land and people prosper.

Studies show they are mentally healthier than other people in the world (Saints not Ain'ts). The world won't share this fact with you, but the Born Again thought process is stable and unique.

Stay focused on Him for **Perfect Peace**. Keep your mind on Him. This must be possible or else He would not have said it.

September 10

Mark 5:15

"And they came to Jesus and see him that was possessed with the devil, and had the legion, sitting and clothed and in his right mind and they were afraid."

Mental challenges? 90% of your problems are already solved. Actually 100%, because God can even help those that are medically unstable.

What about those whose minds are in such chaos, they are too weak to pray for themselves? Enter the Priesthood.

A priest represents God and man. Standing for man is called intercession or standing in the gap. The priest cries out to God on man's behalf until he is free. Note people were afraid of him. Because he was in his right mind.

Yes, you are a peculiar but a mighty people and He is a mind regulator.!

September 11

John 6:66

"From that time many of his disciples went back and walked no more with him."

Six is the number of man and is directly under the number seven which is the number of God, which equals completion. Note how this reads (666). It says that many followers would turn back (the spirit of the Anti-Christ).

He knew the ones who would return to the world.

Saints! These are the last days. Now is not the time to become double minded. God is rounding up His people. He is speaking by dreams and visions.

Speaking to you? Then pay **Attention**!

September 12

Luke 21:36

"WATCH ye therefore and pray always that ye may be accounted worthy to escape."

This verse is speaking of the Last Days but also applies to our current personal lives. Beware that you won't be swallowed up by stepping in the same dark hole someone else fell into. Pray and Watch.

The enemy fears those that walk with open eyes while talking with God. Know you are armed and dangerous to hell because you are showing others the Way as well.

God has said He's made you worthy to escape!

September 13

Hosea 4:6

"My people are destroyed for lack of knowledge."

Human nature tends to be self-centered even in soul winning. We forget we are not saved just for ourselves but for others as well.

We should be armed with knowledge even when that particular subject or sin does not apply to us. We need to be prepared to answer every man about our faith so that others may find the WAY too.

Do not shut down information because that's not your experience, but be equipped to answer every man!

September 14

Matthew 3:2

"Repent for the kingdom of God is at hand."

Picture humanity headed in one direction. Some see the sign **Repent** and understand that word means to turn around, go the other way. Some disregard and keep heading the wrong way.

Many are invited into the Kingdom reading the sign overhead which reads "Chosen from the foundation of the world."

God knew you would choose wisely.

So breathe and know **JESUS** is the WAY and the **DOOR!**

At hand means it is available to you right now!

September 15

Revelation 3:18

*"Anoint your eyes with eye salve
that you may see."*

Often Christians walk out of church Sunday morning still blind and unchanged, while storing up more information about the Kingdom of God, never to experience its power,

This Sunday go expecting: "Lord we understand faith comes by hearing but today we pray your Holy Spirit helps us to focus and experience your divine power as well as hear about it."

"Speak through your shepherds everywhere this Sunday that your people may hear."

September 16

Ephesians 1:21

"Far above all principality, power, might, domain and every name... Not only in this world to come."

Rejoice and realize God created you a being of strength, ability and power above all circumstances. **They all work for your good.**

Others may not know who you are but the great I AM knows and loves you dearly.

This revelation will cause you to begin fixing your own life – a BLESSING going somewhere to happen, quietly moving and touching lives of others.

September 17

Isaiah 3:10

"Say to the righteous that it shall be well with them."

We are blessed to know the promises of God are not fairy tales but really will end happily **Ever After.** Know with God's intervention things turn out the way they are supposed to. Don't expect the worse to happen, expect the best.

Your Father says it will be well with you.

If you question if you are one of the righteous, ask the Lord why or ask someone to explain.

If you already know, then fix it!

September 18

Isaiah 36:11-12

"They held their peace and answered him not a word."

The king of Assyria was talking mess to the Jews about a wall they were building for their own protection and challenging them about their God in Hebrew. But their king commanded them not to talk to him. Your enemy knows your personal language and how to tempt and get you to doubt God.

Let the devil know you cannot be reasoned with. For your own protection hold no conversation with him. He lies.

God is for you!

September 19

Romans 13:14

"We walk by faith, not by sight."

Do not work failure into your plans by saying "If my business fails I can always file bankruptcy or If God doesn't heal me, I have insurance."

No general ever goes into battle planning to lose. What do you see at the inception of your dreams? Shut the door, keep out the devil, then gaze into the Kingdom of God and plan to win.

Line your hearts and pockets with IN GOD WE TRUST!

September 20

Psalms 34:17-22

"The righteous cry and the Lord hears them;
He is near the broken hearted
and saves those of contrite spirit.
A righteous man may have many troubles,
but the Lord delivers him from them ALL."

Those who take refuge in Him will not be condemned.

Gotta love a God like that!

September 21

John 10:10

"The thief comes to steal, kill and destroy."

The worst thing that could happen to an individual or society is to lose **HOPE**. When missionaries went to Africa they taught them about Jesus, but miracles were not for today. So when they got sick, they went back to witchcraft and voodoo.

They were robbed of hope and their rich inheritance.

Wherever you are today Hope in God. He still answers prayers and performs miracles!

September 22

Numbers 13:30

"They said we should by all means go up and take possession of the land, for we will surely overcome."

You are not called to simply exist in a safe environment (Holy Bench Warmers). You are called to reach out of your comfort zone, take risks, pray and move upward.

Do you have concrete plans for fulfilling your vision? Have you taken any steps towards it?

Let's move forward with Joshua and Caleb kind of faith. Step up to that vision and plan to take possession of it.

September 23

WORDS FOR TODAY:

(1) Minding your own Business = Less Drama.

(2) Pray for someone else besides yourself. Even for those who have hurt you. Pray for their happiness. Happy people don't hurt other people.

(3) Stay faithful and let him use you to bring heaven to earth.

(4) Represent! Observers shouldn't have to guess if you are a Christian.

(5) Claim what is yours. Take it back from the thief!!!

(6) Be Still and Know your God.

September 24

Isaiah 41:10

*"I will uphold you
with my righteous right hand."*

God holds our arms and hands in the midst of battle, assuring victory.

Sometimes our arms fall to our sides. But the Lord says, "I will support you. I will be your victory even when you are tired and grow weary."

So today whatever the war, because He already knows, I speak Victory in FMSM reader's lives today. Against illness, addition and demonic attacks.

No weapon formed against you shall prosper!

September 25

Proverbs 8:17-21

"That I may cause those that love Me to inherit substance; and I will fill their treasure."

This series will be on **Prosperity:**

This verse says when you love the Lord and seek out His desires and plans, you will not have to hunt down prosperity, and it will look you up.

I pray today for understanding and that your relationship with Him blossoms into something beyond your wildest dreams.

It's to our benefit to know and trust our God!

September 26

I Corinthians *2:9*

"eye hath not seen nor heard, neither have entered into the heart of man the things which god has prepared for them that love him."

How do I love him like that? Like you would begin any other relationship. He knows if you spend time and get to know Him, you will fall in love with Him. Who do you love with such intensity that they occupy your mental time. Who is it that you demand respect from when others mention your loved one?

Joy and Blessings to those hearts that are near to Him.

Hallelujah!

September 27

Genesis 24:40

"The Lord before whom I walk will send his angel with thee and prosper thy way."

As you walk before the Lord, fall in love and begin to understand His true nature. Angels walk in front of you to prepare your way, behind you to protect you from what you cannot see and beside you for your comfort and company.

This is the kind of God we serve. He has sent His angels today to protect and prosper you.

So Believe Him!

September 28

Genesis 39:3

"His master saw that the Lord was with him and that the Lord made all that he did to prosper in his hand."

Prosperity = All needs met by God. Because you are His, it is God's will for you to prosper in your mind first and your pockets as well.

Often people cannot see your heart, but they see your life style.

Also that your cabinets and freezer are never empty regardless the state of the world's economy.

May the readers of these devotionals prosper in everything they put their hands to, so that others will see the Lord is with you and are highly favored.

September 29

I Timothy 6:10

"The love of money is the root of all evil."

Note: money is not the culprit here, but the love of it. As we continue with this series on prosperity, let's make it clear that God wants His people to be prosperous.

Yes, the world has riches but what are they doing with it? Plans for power and evil or for giving and helping others? Also know you cannot buy miracles.

This week let's be **Still** and **Know!** Make plans for the wealth our Father wants us to have, careful not to lose focus on why. It has to be to His glory not ours.

Holy Spirit guide us!

September 30

Proverbs 29:2

"When the righteous are in authority the people rejoice: but when the wicked rule the people mourn."

It is a fact whenever God receives recognition, that nation thrives.

Another reason creation awaits Sons of God to claim their inheritance. Imagine a world were people know there is no lack so there is no need to steal, kill or destroy. This is why the wealth of the wicked is stored up for the righteous.

Be Still and Know!

Thoughts

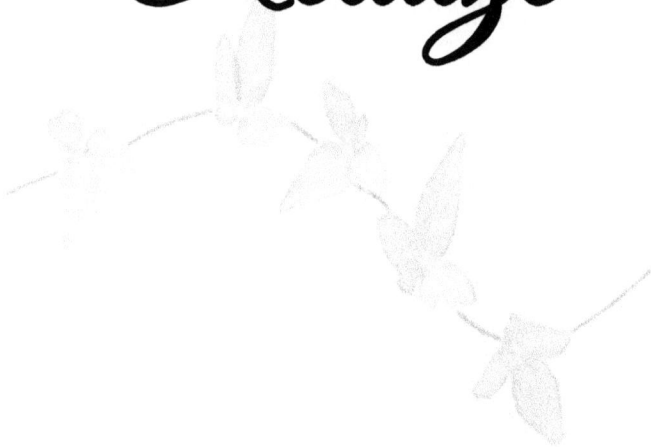

October 1

Job 36:11

*"If they obey and serve Him,
they shall spend their years in prosperity and
their year in pleasures."*

Think back on times you spent being ignorant or willfully disobedient to God. How'd that work for ya? What would you do differently?

There is a powerful promise in this word today.

Let us obey and get our acts together. We have a work to do. Getting folks into the kingdom by showing forth His love and glory.

They need to see how He treats his children!

October 2

Joshua 1:7

"Turn not from it to the right hand or to the left that you may prosper where ever you go."

Again we see God's heart and personality. He promises that if we remain loyal to Him, he will bless where ever we go.

Holy Spirit give us witty ideas that people in our immediate surroundings know we are supernaturally blessed from on High!

October 3

Psalms 1:3

"He shall be like a tree
planted by the rivers of water that bring forth
his fruit in his season, his leaf also shall not
wither and whatsoever he does shall
PROSPER."

Those who are taking this series seriously, the Holy Spirit has given you ideas how to prosper. Pay attention, write your vision, see it manifest.

It is **NOW** our season Sons of God!

October 4

Romans 12:2

"Be transformed by the renewing of your mind."

You can not give a loaded gun to a child. Money is a loaded gun for some. Great power comes with wealth. We need to know how to handle money while keeping Jesus on the throne of our hearts. This is easier said than done. We have to keep checking our hearts by renewing our minds daily.

If we can't keep God first with what we have now, how can He trust us later with more?

We must have a Made-Up mind.

BE STILL AND KNOW!

October 5

Romans 10:17

"Faith comes by hearing and hearing by the word of God."

Today based on Psalms 66:12 speak these words out loud to yourself so that your spirit hears and reacts based on your confessions:

The Lord has brought me out into a wealthy place. He protects me keeps me when enemies attack. Keeps me through fiery trials and dangerous circumstances that seek to destroy my life by temptation. Through it all God will bring me into a wealthy place.

Be still and **KNOW!**

October 6

Proverbs 10:22

"The blessing of the Lord, it makes rich, and He adds no sorrow with it."

When blessings are from God, He does not take it back. He won't bring hardship with it.

Say these words to yourself today:

I will not be poor. God's blessing is upon me, my family and community because I will not use it for evil.

It is time we **KNOW!**

October 7

Psalms 1:3

"And he shall be like a tree planted by the rivers of water, that brings forth his fruit in his season; his leaf also shall not wither and whatsoever he does shall PROSPER."

Speak these words to your heart today:

My time has come. I will see great results produced in my life and business. I will be strong. Because I am obedient to God's Word, I will not wither under pressure and whatever I do shall PROSPER and last forever.

Be still and **KNOW**!

October 8

Ecclesiastes 11:6

"In the morning sow your seed
and in the evening withhold not your hand
for thou knowest not your hand for thou
knowest not whether shall prosper,
either this or that or whether they both shall be
alike good."

I may not know my last days here on earth, but I do know I will always prosper because I am a sower and a giver.

I do not worry about the seed I sow. Just like a farmer I know at all times some portion of my seed will take root, grow and give me a harvest providing more seed which will grant even more opportunity to prosper.

Be still and **KNOW!**

October 9

Isaiah 45:3

*"I will give you the treasures of darkness
and hidden riches of secret places that you
may know that I the Lord
which call you your name
am the God of Israel."*

Say these words:

*There is treasure I cannot see. There are riches
hidden in secret places. God knows where they
are and has promised to give them to me.*

*God grants me access to these things because I
am one of His Called Ones. He wants me to
know that He will provide for my every need.*

Be still and **KNOW**!

October 10

Ezekiel 28:4

"With your wisdom and with your understanding thou has gotten thee riches and has gotten gold and silver into thy treasures:"

I do not seek after gold and silver. I seek after wisdom and understanding. They are my two good friends. They will bring me abundance and prosperity in every area of my life.

The Lord is my shepherd. I shall not want, I lack nothing.

This concludes the series on prosperity. I pray it expels any doubt as to what God wants for you. I didn't mention tithes on purpose. I figured your local pastor has educated you on that subject numerous times.

Have a Blessed and Prosperous day!

October 11

Psalms 23:9

*"Speak not in the ears of a fool,
for he will despise the wisdom of thy words."*

Sometimes there is no need to fix burned bridges. Check your own heart. God may have burned them. The Word says to shake the dust off your feet and keep moving. Leave it alone, then face forward in love. While planting and watering new seeds, don't look back.

It is all in His mighty hands. He knows exactly how and what to do with them.

This year, find PEACE in this Truth.

October 12

Job 14:14

"I will wait til my change comes."

Job expected change in his circumstances. We too are engaged in a fight of faith. Our warfare against the powers of darkness goes on and on.

However, like Job we can expect dramatic changes in our lives and the church world.

Look forward to them. He is calling His children together from every corner of the world in victory. So hold on until your change comes.

In spite of what it looks like, you have something to look forward to.

Rejoice again I say Rejoice!

October 13

Isaiah 33:10

"NOW I will rise says the Lord; NOW I will be exalted, NOW I will lift Myself up."

God is the great I AM. We can't increase Him with our words but we can decrease Him with them in our hearts.

When we magnify our circumstances and problems we downsize the Lord and His ability to help us. When we magnify the Lord with our praise, He says, "NOW I will move. NOW I will lift Myself up on your behalf."

This is why the enemy hates the power of your praise and worship.

Oh magnify the Lord. Who is like Him?

October 14

Job 33:15-16

*"In a dream, in a vision of the night,
when deep sleep falls upon men, while
slumbering on their beds, then he opens the
ears of me,
and seals their instruction."*

This tells us that God is going to speak to us in dreams and visions.

In the night when deep sleep falls upon us, He will open our ears to hear. He will seal up our instruction. He will even warn us if need be.

All through the sleep process. How will you know it was Him?

Your spirit and His word will bear witness.

October 15

Luke 8:5-8

"Some fell by the wayside on rocks, thorns and others fell on good ground."

Seed = Word of God. Ground = the heart.

Sometimes we feel like a nut. Sometimes we don't. On fire one day, running from His presence the next. We blame others or too ashamed to approach Him, knowing we haven't been faithful.

Why? Because we have no respect or fear for of His power.

He is not expecting perfection, but He does desire our loyalty. Stop trusting emotions. They'll only mislead you.

Check the ground, see if your heart is fertile.

October 16

Proverbs 17:27

"A man of understanding has a cool spirit."

In today's society, to be cool means street wise, confident. He listens to cool music and hangs with other cool people who wear cool clothes.

The truly spiritual person is cool because he understands he has blessed assurance. He knows his God is jealously watching over him. So he's not quick to lose his temper or believe bad reports. He is quiet, calm and composed in His spirit.

Let us learn to swag the Bible way.

October 17

Psalms 119:165

"Great peace have those who love your law and nothing causes them to stumble."

Filling our hearts with the Word of God is the only sure way to overcome enemy ambushes. This great peace promise is so profound that with it in our hearts we are assured of passing safely through all danger zones without stumbling into temptations. Come what may, we can walk in confidence and great peace 24 hours a day!

Make it a habit to daily hide His Word in your heart.

October 18

James 1:22

"Be doers of the Word and not hearers only, deceiving your own selves."

Some people are playing themselves, believing they are true Christians. However, they will throw God under the bus in a heartbeat, in order to carry out their own desires.

It's an easy road to wrong. They bow down, but only to the Altar of Self. **Galatians 6:7** "Don't be deceived, God is not mocked."

Let us examine our relationship with our Father today.

We should examine ourselves and ask, do we even have one?

October 19

Romans 12:12

"Continuing instant in prayer:"

This series is entitled" **The Power of Praying in Tongues.**

Prayer is *Spirit to Spirit* communication. Many believers know this fact in their heads, but they do not know it as a living experience. This is why there is little manifestation of Power in their lives.

It is not the will of God that you walk in little power when all His ability is available to you - not some but All!

May this series awaken the power of God in you!

October 20

I Thessalonians 5:17

"Pray without ceasing."

Prayer means to make an intervention. To come in between to prevent or alter results or events.

Stepping in the middle to stop an oncoming attack.

To a believer who desires the supernatural edge, it is imperative that you develop a strong prayer life. There is a direct connection between prayer and power.

If you are going to grow in the anointing, it is of the utmost importance that you develop a strong prayer life.

October 21

I Corinthians 14:18

"Paul said, "I thank my God I speak with tongues more than you all."

This was the secret to Paul's supernatural life, revelations and ministry.

There are two kinds of Spirit-led prayer. One is done with the mind engaged in your unknown tongue and the other with the mind by passed.

Praying in the spirit is praying your heavenly language of tongues.

If the Lord said the believer will speak with new tongues, then the matter is settled.

October 22

Mark 16:15-17

"These signs shall follow them that believe; In my name shall they cast out devils; they shall speak with new tongues."

When you became a born-again believer, you are a brand new species that never ever existed before.

Likewise, speaking in tongues is a brand new thing that never existed before. Speaking or praying in tongues was and is a new phenomenon that belongs to believers on this side of the cross and resurrection.

You are not of this world (NOTW)!

October 23

I Corinthians 12:1

"Concerning spiritual gifts brethren,
I would not have you ignorant."

The supernatural and the realm of the miracles are for the believer. Witchcraft, psychics tarot card readers, fortune telling, wizards and New Agers are not the inventers of and do not monopolize the supernatural.

What the occult calls supernatural is demonic infestation.

The supernatural and miraculous are for the believer.

Have a wonderful blessed day!

October 24

Acts 2:4

"Were all filled with the Holy Ghost and began to speak with other tongues."

Tongues has nothing to do with your salvation or having the Holy Spirit.

When you receive salvation, you become the temple of the Holy Spirit. As a born again child of God, the Holy Spirit is already inside you, living in your life.

The baptism of the Holy Spirit with tongues is another blessing altogether.

Not every believer has been baptized in the Holy Spirit. Why?

October 25

Acts 1:8

*"But ye shall receive POWER after that
the Holy Ghost is come upon you:
and ye shall be witnesses unto me."*

If the Holy Ghost resides in all believers, why
must we be baptized in the Holy Spirit?

His audience at that time were believers. Yet He
told them they would receive power.

You were saved when you confessed with your
MOUTH and believed with your HEART. We
need the Baptism by Fire for Power. **Note**: He
did not say by water.

This endowment of power renders the believer
fit for service to God. You do not need tongues
to be saved, but you cannot receive the Baptism
of the Holy Spirit without first receiving
salvation.

October 26

I Corinthians 14:2

*"For he that speaks in an unknown tongue
speaks not unto men but unto God:
for no man understands him;
howbeit in the spirit he speaks mysteries."*

Praying in tongues is the gateway into the spirit realm.

Notice the words 'howbeit in the spirit'. In other words, when you start praying in tongues, you are entering God's miracle zone.

Tongues are the key that unlock the spirit world. As long as Satan can keep you away from tongues, he can keep you away from miracles.

October 27

I Corinthians 14:2

"Speaks not unto men but to God."

Millions of people all over the world would like an audience with God and doing all kinds of silly things like piercing their bodies, lighting candles, offering all kinds of sacrifices for this purpose. They may reach something, but it will not be God.

However, when believers pray in the spirit, Satan understands what they are doing, but he is helpless to sabotage their prayer, because he can not understand the language because it is an A and B conversation.

Tongues is the believer's direct access to the throne room.

October 28

Those who are seeking their own divine prayer language know it is a matter of faith, but you have to open your mouth, meaning you must let the Holy Spirit take control of your tongue.

It does not have to be a church setting, but must be a matter of faith and your heart, not what is said.

The safest way is to start is with praise, such as hallelujah until you hear yourself speaking another language. Do not try to fix it, let it go. No matter how it sounds relax and continue.

Know the enemy will tell you that you made that up, but most important, God understands and knows your heart.

October 29

I Corinthians 2:7

"We speak the wisdom of God in a mystery."

The anointing is strong when you are in the plan and will of God for your life. The plan of God is that divine direction for your life, ministry, job or any area of your life, will be revealed to you as you pray in the Holy Ghost.

Even when we know the plan, sometimes we don't know how to implement or how to get it done. This is why we pray in the Holy Ghost to get step-by-step instructions that leads to the overall plan.

The Word encourages you if haven't already to speak to Him in your heavenly language.

October 30

I Corinthians 14:4

"He that speaks in an unknown tongue edifies himself."

Paul was telling the Corinthian church to keep praying and worshiping in tongues as a means of spiritual edification which means to build or improve.

We all could improve in some way. Might say home improvement. Edify also means to charge you up like you would a battery. Tongues is building a strong premise to carry the anointing. A spiritual current.

Why wouldn't someone want to improve?

October 31

Jude 1:20

"Building up yourselves on your most holy faith, praying in the Holy Ghost."

Tongues stimulates your faith. Jude warns of a time of great apostasy in the last days when right will be considered wrong and vice versa. There would be tough times. What we need in these days is strong and stimulated faith.

As you pray your progress will become unstoppable and undeniable by your worst enemies.

Learn to pray and worship, even in your worst times.

Thoughts

November 1

Acts 10:46

*"They heard them speak with tongues
and magnify God."*

Apart from meaning praise and thanksgiving to God, **magnify** in this text also means to increase in size and capacity.

When you pray in tongues, God is getting bigger and bigger on the inside of you. Your perception of God changes and increases.

The bigger God gets in your life, the smaller the devil will be.

Tongues will enlarge your faith!

November 2

Isaiah 28:11-12

"With stammering lips and another tongue
will He speak to His people.
To whom He said this is the rest wherewith you
may cause the weary rest,
and this is the refreshing."

Note this verse says He will speak to His people.

Tongues will give you rest in the midst of warfare. This is how Paul kept himself strong, refreshed and on the cutting edge when all hell was assigned to him.

He constantly prayed in tongues and thanked God that he did more than the Corinthian church without apology.

This prayer language is for believers, not unbelievers, for they will think you are crazy. Some other person should interpret (**I Corinthians 14:23**).

Otherwise this should be done in private.

November 3

Proverbs 18:21

"Death and life are in the power of the tongue."

Control your tongue and you will control your life. Praying in tongues will keep you from profane, vulgar and obscene communication.

When you develop the habit of praying in tongues you will not gossip, tell dirty jokes or be involved in any other filthy communication.

Tongues is not repeating two or three same words over and over again, but an actual language.

November 4

Psalms 42:7

"Deep calls unto deep."

It is difficult to deepen a relationship with someone if you both speak different languages. The lack of understanding becomes a major barrier to a deep, meaningful relationship.

Speaking God's language will enable you to deepen your relationship with Him. Never forget how deep you go with God will determine how high you will go in life. From glory to glory.

"Acquaint now thyself with Him and be at peace thereby good shall come to thee." (Job 22:21)

November 5

I Thessalonians 5:17

"Pray without ceasing."

Tongues enables us to pray much.

While there are many kinds of prayer, tongues is the ability to pray any time without running out of words - permitting you to stay in prayer for long periods of time.

While speaking in tongues the mind is not taxed and can focus while the spirit prays.

Wow! God thought of everything!

November 6

Isaiah 47:13

"Let your astrologers come forth,
those stargazers who make monthly predictions,
let them save you from what's coming."

As stated in previous text you are a new creation. Your sign is the sign of the CROSS. You are not limited by a star planet. The God who lives in you is not bound by any.

Refuse to let anyone keep you in chains or a box by insisting you claim a sign.

You are Holy Kings, a Royal Priesthood. Jesus shed his blood so that you would not have to live cursed. Something is coming and will not be able to help you.

In these last days, God will say, "How did that work for you Boo?"

Let not his blood be in vain and work in your behalf.

November 7

Psalms 107:35

"He turneth the wilderness into standing water springs."

Don't be so sure it was the devil who lured you into the wilderness.

Even in those dry places where God is silent, He is watching with a protective eye.

There, is where He allows you to blossom into tender desert flowers. That desert will yield water springs.

You may have been lured there by some other expectation. That person is being used to test and grow you up. Just watch, that situation is going to be fruitful if you are one of His.

It's **All GOOD!**

November 8

Romans 8:19

"For the earnest expectation of the creature waits for the manifestation of the sons of God."

Be who you are. If not, it's easy to get sucked into other people's perception of you.

You will be disappointed in yourself, and others will be let down as well, because they need you to be who God intended you to be.

The world is looking for something real not necessarily material.

Until He moves you, grow where you are planted. He will use you there.

November 9

Matthew 14:28

"And Peter answered him and said, Lord, if it be thou, bid me come unto thee on the water. And he said Come. And Peter was come down out of the ship, he walked on the water to go Jesus."

Keep God's promises before you just as Peter obeyed Jesus and walked on water, he began to sink when he took his eyes off Jesus. Doubt took over his mind.

In fact, it was Peter who said, "If it is you bid me to come to you." Jesus answered keeping His part of the bargain. It was Peter who lost focus by looking at circumstances or problem.

Problem: it was humanly impossible for man to walk on water.

When brick walls occur in your life, know with God all things are possible. Lord we believe you for healing, finances and favor today.

November 10

I Corinthians 10:5

"Bringing into captivity every thought to the obedience of Christ."

Time for A mind check:

STOP! What is your mind up to right Now? Is it in a state of belief or fretting and worrying? Is it angry or does it know God will fight its battles?

Command it to know and understand God is your Source. What is it doing? Stable or just tripping?

Start right NOW to begin the day in victory by changing its way of viewing things.

Speak to that mountain that it may MOVE!

November 11

Romans 2:3

*"Think thou this… that judgest them
which do such things and do the same,
that thou shall escape the judgment of God?"*

People use this verse to say we should not judge, but what it really says if you are doing the same thing and are aware of the truth, you have no right to judge and are dammed also.

Matthew 7:16 warns of false prophets "you will know them by their fruits." How will you know if you won't judge the Fruit?

In these last days we need to learn to pray, judge and discern.

November 12

Romans 8:28

"We know all things work together for good to them who love God."

God starts in your future not in your past. He arranges this so that you won't want to go back. He allows things to happen so that you have no option but to go forward.

The enemy is not attacking you on your past, but has glimpsed your future. The only thing he can do is keep reminding you of your past mistakes and worries. He doesn't know the deepest parts of your heart but observes how you respond to life.

His worst move is to try and take you out. This only gives God reason to take you up and over!

November 13

Isaiah 42:16

"I will bring the blind by a way they knew not."

Don't fret over what could or should have been because you did the best you could with the understanding you had. Did you really know hell was real?

The safest place to be is to tell God you don't know where you are going because if you knew where you were going you wouldn't need Him.

It takes revelation to know you can't see. This is the beginning of spiritual sight.

We need you Lord. Open our eyes Holy Spirit!

November 14

Psalms 100:4

"Enter into his gates with thanksgiving and into his courts with praise."

Scripture tells us how to enter into God's presence. Gratitude is also a powerful weapon against your enemy.

Here is where he cannot conquer you, because faith and doubt cannot occupy the same space.

Here you stand in victory. God finds pleasure in your thanksgiving. So wherever you find yourself today, give thanks to your Father even for the little things.

We love and thank you Lord.

November 15

Psalms 91:1

*"He that dwells in the secret place
of the most High shall abide under the shadow
of the Almighty."*

There is something about a dwelling place. Know its purpose.

When you walk in fear, you walk out of the presence of God, then you try to fix it yourself.

The enemy wants you to stay in control. Find your way to God's resting place. The Secret Place. In Him you will find security.

Prayer, Word, thanksgiving and Worship is the way you stay in His presence.

November 16

Proverbs 25:28

"He that has no rule over his own spirit is like a city that is broken down and without walls."

Are you living your life by the decisions of others? Are you accomplishing goals that are your own?

There will be times you need to take uncalculated risks as a child who trusts.

You can't count on anyone/anything to be safe. You just have to know God is your ultimate Source. This takes a made-up mind to have rule over your own spirit.

He won't ask the impossible.

That's His job!

November 17

Isaiah 43:18-19

"DO NOT remember the former things, nor consider the things of old. Behold, I will do a <u>new</u> thing. NOW it shall spring forth."

This Word literally commands us to leave the past and get ready for the future. The Lord has new things for you.

It is impossible to look in two directions at the same time. Lingering in past memories, good, bad, could cause you to pass up the new things and miss out on the good things, He has planned for you.

Just *Let It Go* Man!

November 18

I Corinthians 12:8-9

"To another... special faith."

This Word promises us that we do not have to be anxious or insecure about the days to come. The gift of faith confidently states "God has met us in the past, He is meeting us in the present and we know by faith, He will meet us in the future."

It is the God-given ability to trust your situation into His hands and see Him work it out for you, comfort you. All for His glory.

Special faith is yours for the asking!

November 19

Luke 17:14

"When he saw them he said to them,
go show yourselves to the priest.
It came to pass <u>as they went</u>
they were cleansed."

When Jesus told the ten lepers to go show themselves to the priest, their outward appearance remained the same. But by the time they reached their destination they were healed.

He does not operate on our time table and may let you go through before manifestation. Know as you walk with Him, He is doing a work in you, spiritually and physically.

If things appear the same, hang in there!

November 20

Matthew 8:19

*"A teacher of the law came to him and said;
Teacher, I will follow you wherever you go."*

Only a disciple experiences full potential
because his greatest desire is to know and look
like his Master.

He spends hours listening to his words. Getting
to know and understand Him, developing
kingdom mentality.

Do not let the world deceive you with its
limitations.

Find your Source and stay connected!

November 21

Isaiah 55:11

*"My word that goes from my mouth,
it will not return to me empty but accomplish
what I desire and achieve the purpose
for which I sent it."*

Know you are a speaking spirit made in the image of God Himself. Words you speak will not return to you void either.

Watch what you say today because some of the words you speak, you may **want** them to return void.

Don't always rely on the fact that God is merciful, knowing you can be a child with a loaded pistol.

He may let something manifest out of your mouth, so you will realize how powerful He has made you.

November 22

Isaiah 40:31

"They shall mount up as eagles."

FLYING LESSONS:

Viewing things from a higher altitude appear much smaller when you draw near to God. The devil and problems look ridiculous and small when compared to your Father.

Come up higher and trust Him to show you wonderful things. He won't drop you. You will not fall.

The earth is the Lord's and the fullness thereof. FEAR NOT, talk with Him and come closer. Power is knowing the Creator of the universe is in love with you.

So Mount Up and Fly!

November 23

Matthew 26:41

"Watch and pray that you enter not into temptation, the spirit indeed is willing but the flesh is weak."

It is natural wanting to make others happy. But it's different when that need to show love turns into worship of God's creations.

Our worship should be horizontal rather than vertical. When committing an act of service and not expecting payback or recognition, you know your worship is in check.

Even then be careful not to become self righteous in your own eyes.

Watch and Pray!

November 24

Proverbs 8:13

*"The fear of the Lord is to hate evil.
Pride and arrogancy and the evil way
and the forward mouth do I hate."*

You will automatically fear God by hating evil and pride. But hate the pride in yourself first, then you will discern it in others, knowing how to respond, if at all.

God will use you in the realm of humility where your desires will be the same as His, while hating evil.

In this case, it's okay to be a Hater and still be humble.

November 25

Exodus 3:4

"When the Lord saw that he turned aside to See, God called to him out of the midst of the bush and said Moses, Moses and he said, Here am I."

We are to seek His face with all our hearts, soul and mind. Some of us need failure or crisis to finally seek Him out.

At times we need to stop and investigate occurrences in our lives to see what God is trying to show us. Unemployment, broken relationships, etc. may be burning bushes.

Tell God, "Here I am."

Then **Stop**, be **Still** and **Listen**!

November 26

Deuteronomy 4:24

"The Lord your God is a consuming fire, a jealous God."

TWO LOVERS:

We may find ourselves torn between what the world can offer as opposed to God, but in the end we have to come back admitting, can't nobody do me like Jesus.

While flirting with the other lover, you might conceive something you hadn't counted on. The world can be cold blooded. You will lose your soul, money, friends, etc.

Look back on those times, repent and let the lover of your soul birth new things in you. He has made a new day just for you.

Rejoice and be glad in it!

November 27

Zechariah 2:8

"For he that touches you,
touches the apple of his eye."

The word says before the foundation of the earth, you were chosen by Him. You are very special. The Word says you are the Apple of His eye. The apple of the eye is the pupil, so vital to sight that the body protects it without an order to the brain.

If anything hurtles towards you, your eye automatically shuts.

Take a deep breath and breathe. Remember, demons don't gather around closed doors. Why would they?

The next time a door slams shut, it just might be your Father has blinked, automatically protecting the **Apple** of His **Eye**.

November 28

John 15:15

"Henceforth I call you not servants;
for the servant knows not what his lord doeth:
but I have called you friends;
for all things that I have heard of my Father
I have made known unto you."

Good friends are hard to find. Cherish them.
Notice these friends were servants first. At some
point in their growth process they became
friends with God and He shared everything he
knew.

The Great I Am has called them Friends. Can
you imagine that? Enoch didn't even die. God
took him. That's how close they were.

God has servants but few friends. Let us strive to
be a good friend as well! Let our hearts desire
for Him to know He can trust us.

Talk to Him.

November 29

Ezekiel 37:10

"So I prophesied as he commanded me and the breath came into them and they lived and stood on their feet an exceeding army."

When you speak the word of God, words that come out of your mouth form a **mighty army**. The Holy Spirit, angelic host and Jesus the High Priest agree and war over your words and are activated.

Put flesh and breathe upon those dry bones by speaking and believing what He has said. Things you prophesy over will assemble themselves into a great army.

Your words are building material.

November 30

Isaiah 55:8

"My thoughts are not your thoughts, neither are your ways says the Lord."

When prophesying, make sure you and God agree.

Satan understood the principal of speaking, but he hadn't a clue about *agreement* or he would never had said things like, "I will be like the Most High."

GOD did not agree. He had another idea: A spirit made in His image able to speak things into existence like Himself.

Satan hates you for this reason. So speak over your life and family.

Thoughts

December 1

Matthew 5:6

"Blessed are they which do hunger and thirst after righteousness for they shall be filled."

Time for a heart examination:

What is your heart up to? Is it hungering and thirsting for God with all its might? Is it willing to give Him the sacrifice of praise no matter what it is going through now?

This is how we hunger and thirst for Him. What are we willing to do, to be in His presence?

To make it in these LAST DAYS we must stay HUNGRY!

Everything about this walk is about our heart.

December 2

Luke 22:31

"Simon behold Satan has desired to have you so he may sift you as wheat."

The devil wanted to destroy Peter but Jesus had prayed for him. The devil needed the okay from God and He allowed it because Peter had to have pride purged out of him, but the outcome was already spoken by the WORD that Peter would pastor the first church.

Again the enemy hadn't thought it through, but it if it hadn't been in Peter's heart he would not have been able to test him. God knew what was in his heart, but Peter needed to know for himself.

If God be for you, who can be against you?

December 3

II Corinthians 1:20

"For all the promises of God in Him are yea and Amen."

We are not dumb enough, smart enough, crazy or powerful enough to stop the promises of God.

The enemy does not want you to read God's Word or talking to Him about it, because the Holy Spirit will reveal your destiny. Hell has a destiny as well, it's nothing nice.

Stay in the Word repeating His promises aloud. Hearing yourself echo what He has said about you. Such as, you are a 'lender not a borrower, etc.'

Faith comes by hearing!

December 4

I Corinthians 13:1-2

*"Though I speak with the tongues of men
and angels and have not love,
I am as a sounding brass or tinkling cymbal."*

Many of you are called to ministry. However, be careful how you treat God's people or some poor soul who needs Christ only to get you instead.

Using your gift for recognition is not acceptable! It's like trying to cash a check that's not yours.

This is forgery.

"Many will say to me in that day, Lord have we not prophesied in your name? And in thy name have cast out devils? And then I will profess unto them, I never knew you. Depart from me ye that work inequity." (**Matthew 7:22**)

How embarrassing!

December 5

I Kings 19:4

"He requested for himself that he might die and said it's enough; now Lord take my Life."

After a victory or accomplishment in Christ is when you really need to be aware and sensitive to the attacks of hell.

Elijah just had many victories over Jezebel, but when she threatened to kill him, he went into a state of depression, forgetting quickly what miracles were performed on his behalf.

Never get caught with your guard down. Soldiers of God stay dressed for battle.

December 6

Genesis 3:14

"Who told you that you were naked?

Who said you couldn't talk to me, now that you've messed up? You ran from Me, Remember?

Who said you're too fat, too old, and not pretty enough, your race is dumb, or you'll always be on drugs?

Don't you dare let anyone speak shame into your life and relationship with your Father.

The WORD says you are new creatures and you can do all thing through Christ. Stop making comparisons and realize God put something into your hand that's unlike anyone else.

It's unique and tailor made just for you!

December 7

I Kings 19:12

"After the earthquake a fire
but the Lord was not in the fire
and after the fire a Still Small Voice."

Thoughts try to crowd and yell at the forefront of your mind when distressed to get your attention. However, in the back of the crowd, the Holy Spirit waits patiently until invited forward, speaking in a **still small voice** to guide you through your turmoil.

Trust will part the sea of those stressful thoughts and make way for Peace to enter in.

Be still and know He's there.

December 8

Romans 16:20

"The God of peace shall bruise Satan under your feet shortly."

Satan is beneath your feet. You are not under any circumstance unless you crawl under it.

Wherever you are this day tell your self the truth about the situation. Remind God of what He said about it.

He loves it. That means you were listening!

Employment seekers, didn't He say that He is **Jehovah Jireh** your provider? You are above not beneath? He would prepare a table in front of your enemies? No weapon formed against you would prosper? Who is like our GOD?

He is the God who heals, even your broken heart.

December 9

Psalms 32:8

***"The Lord says
I will make you wise and show you where to go.
I will guide you and watch over you."***

Have you ever done something stupid because you did not heed the still small voice of the Lord or His written WORD? Later thinking, "Oh! That meant me too?"

God knew in time you would succumb to the *spirit of dumb*.

Forgive yourself and when you leave the *land of slow* bring nothing with you but lessons learned.

He promised He would guide you through if you repent and obey.

December 10

Matthew 6:10

"Thy kingdom come.
Thy will be done in earth as it is in heaven."

Young people, yesterday we spoke on exiting the *Land of Slow*. You can be a citizen there so long, you aren't even aware you've been living there.

Check out your surroundings and neighbors. What kind of fruit grows there?

There's an old saying if you have 10 dumb friends, what does that make you? The **eleventh**.

If you are reading these messages, you are exposed to more information than a lot of us had at your age.

Decide in your mind NOW, you will not let the devil make a fool of you anymore - not one more day. You have the option to relocate to the Kingdom of Heaven.

December 11

Psalms 115:5

"Eyes have they but see not."

The U.S. Military uses night gear enabling them to see the enemy at night. One eye is attached to a scope for seeing in darkness while the other is used for natural sight.

Because you are a solider of God you have the capability of seeing with your natural eye and in the **Spirit** = **discernment**

You will experience dark times but you are armed with the Spirit of Truth and will be able to see and react to the enemy's motives and intents.

December 12

John 12:35

"For he that walk in darkness know not where he's going."

There are no rules in darkness.

Everybody is fair game. Darkness can be considered the hardening of the heart. In darkness there is a drive to fulfill the lust of the flesh, also causing depression, especially if one knows the Truth.

What helps in these times is to find someone to help. This gets the mind off self instead of the world's code, me! Me!

Other times we must allow TIME to heal before the Light.

December 13

Isaiah 56:6

"Seek the Lord while He may be found. Call upon Him while He is near."

Seek = beating a path or to go over an area so often it rubs smooth.
FOUND = discovered/located.

Any effort to meet the Lord will be met with success. NEAR = nearby vicinity/neighborhood. There are times and seasons when the Lord's presence is especially felt.

Call upon Him while He is near. We are made aware of our own dignity with God's presence in our lives. Holy and set apart becomes clearer.

December 14

Jeremiah 29:11

"I know the thoughts I think towards you say the Lord, thoughts of peace and not of evil to give you an expected end."

We pray and pray and the answer is still NO. We may ask ourselves, "Why pray if God is going to do what He wants anyway?"

The issue is not whether He answers or not. It is whether we believe in His goodness and He loves us.

Know regardless of how it looks it will work out to His glory, and His glory always benefits man.

December 15

Myles Monroe taught on this subject. It blessed me. Hope it blesses you as well.

The prefix Re = to go back to its original state.

REpent: Pent = highest place (example penthouse). To repent means to return to the highest place. The top.

REdeem: Deem = to own. To redeem means to own something twice. We are blood brought

REceive: Ceive = to release. To receive something means to return of what you released.

REturn: Turn = to change the position so the underside becomes the upper side.

From now on, every time you come across these words in scripture take a minute and ponder on them.

December 16

Isaiah: 43:26

"Put me in remembrance: let us plead together: declare thou, that thou mayest be justified."

Praying is not so much asking, as it is confirming. Word says we cannot not please God without faith. When we come before God in prayer, we should be in agreement with His word already believing that what he has promised will be done.

So when you pray, pray God's word back to Him. He says put me in remembrance. He tells us to put Him in remembrance not because he has forgotten what he has promised, but for us to know what he has promised.

Putting Him in remembrance is for your benefit rather than His. Receive His word and pray it back to Him. When that word comes back to Him, it is not void. His word is a container for His thought, which proceeds out of His heart and mind. God's mind is never empty or void.

December 17

Matthew 4:1

"Jesus was led up of the Spirit into the wilderness to be tempted of the devil."

It's not a sin to be tempted. You may be experiencing spiritual opposition because you are doing something right. In fact, if you are not experiencing opposition to your ministry, the devil might not see you as a threat.

You may not see yourself in ministry now, but God has a work for you. You were not saved to sit and observe. You are not meant to be a Holy Bench Warmer!

If you feel under attack, rejoice and cling to God.

Dirt grows things.

December 18

Jeremiah 29:13

"Ye shall seek me and find me when ye shall search for me with all your heart."

If you seek God with all your heart, you cannot be manipulated by man, demon, circumstance - past nor present.

You become that rock that will not move. I pray for each and everyone who is reading this devotional today, that you stand even when it looks like the bottom has fell out and heaven seems quiet.

Stay focused and **Stand** Sons of God, because He is with you!

December 19

I Timothy 1:15

"This is a faithful saying, and worthy of all acceptation, that Christ Jesus came into the world to save sinners; of who I am chief."

You don't wait to go to the doctor or the hospital after you've healed yourself. What would be the point?

If you ever fall, you have every right to plead temporary insanity, because you would have to be out of your mind to listen to the devil who hates you vs. God who loves you. Just as insane knowing that same God also has another side to Him - His wrath. Why would we even want to go there – except we were blinded and insane.

Even though you may be embarrassed or feel you have failed God horribly, it is better to seek His face and repent. Rather than trying to hide, take responsibility for your actions. Return to Him, and He will use it for your growth as well as others' growth.

December 20

Isaiah 5:2

"And he fenced it, and gathered out the stones thereof, and planted it with the choicest vine, and built a tower in the midst of it, and also made a winepress therein: and he looked that it should bring forth grapes, and it brought forth wild grapes."

Beware of favorable conditions. All of us at some time have dealt with tribulation as a child of God.

Living in America is one example of a favorable condition. With little hindrance by the government, we have opportunities to share the Gospel and take it for granted, while our brothers and sisters are being persecuted around the world.

Another may be isolated from friends and loved ones. They find they have a lot of time on their hands. This is the time to seek God and draw closer to Him.

Instead of trying to grow where God has not ordained, or refusing to grow where God has put us, let us labor to bring forth choice fruit rather than wild grapes. All He wants is for us to make ourselves available to Him.

365 REASONS TO STAND TALL

December 21

Genesis 12:1

"The Lord said to Abraham, get out of your country and from your family and from your father's house to the land I will show you."

A vision is only seen by the bearer of it. Because you were chosen to bear it, it will be invisible to others. They will label you by your current state but God knows your potential.

Friends and family are good to have but sometimes they need to be removed for a season.

Surround your self with people who can see beyond your appearance and condition.

Sometimes it's not a physical move, but a mental one.

December 22

Genesis 1:1

"In the beginning"

At the beginning of creation, we not only see the earth in its infancy, but also the beginning of TIME. When God made night and day, time was also created. Everything that was ever created the earth, ministering angels, even time was created for the sake of man.

God has no need of time because He is eternal. He has no beginning and He is without end. The very first sentence, the very first thought he conveys to man is, **In the beginning God**. No explanations or excuses.

Time was created to give man a window of opportunity to repent. To turn around and step into eternity with Him. Would you want to live out of time, eternally out of His presence? That's called Hell. Just as everything else decays and dies, even time will come to an end.

Your problems can't even withstand eternity. Only God's Word is the same yesterday, today and tomorrow.

December 23

Hebrews 4:10

"For he that is entered into his rest, he has also ceased from his own works, God did from His."

Enter into His rest. Sounds easy, but how much do we work trying to solve life's problems ourselves. How much do we rely on government or the school system to legislate hearts?

What about that individual who has decided he cannot live without that other person?

If we stand back a minute, a lot of the weight we carry is self imposed or we have allowed others to dump weights upon us.

We let people stereotype us. Women allow men to exploit them sexually and mentally.

Sometimes we all act like a Jerry Springer guest.

December 24

Philippians 4:4

"Rejoice in the Lord always and again I say Rejoice."

There's that 'R' word again. Why? You may say I really don't feel like rejoicing right now. If you learn to work the Word, it will work for you. Speaking it until you know that you know.

Coming before God rejoicing means you are in great expectation, because you tell Him I believe you Father.

Today say, "I am believing because of you Lord. I am the Righteousness of God." Like a tree by rivers of water... whatsoever he does shall prosper and no weapon formed against us WON'T!

Psalms. 1:2 and *Isaiah 54:17*

December 25

Malachi 3:6

"I am the Lord your God and I never change."

You don't have to be controlled by yesterday. Make yesterday work for you. What did you learn this year? Give yourself permission to move from yesterday because you have a higher calling.

Even though the news has been horrible, God sees and knows all. We may be growing and the world changing but, God remains the same. Because you count on this fact, nothing is getting old for you, except your clothes and your friends.

Stay encouraged. Jesus was born for you and died for you and he is coming back soon!

Merry Christmas!

December 26

II Corinthians 10:3-5

"The weapons of our warfare are not carnal, but mighty through God to the pulling down of strongholds; Casting down imaginations, and every high thing that exalts itself against the knowledge of God, and bringing into captivity every thought to the obedience of Christ."

What is a stronghold? A stronghold is a mind set. Thoughts that control how you respond to the issues of life. A stronghold is a relentless vice grip on the mind that insists upon its own way. This could be good or bad depending on who or what has the stronger hold on your mind.

Negative strongholds are born and thrive in darkness (ignorance). They can torture and make you miserable. They will keep you from the blessings of God, in that you are too weak to trust Him.

To be cont'd

December 27

II Corinthians 10:3-5

"Pulling down strongholds"

Strongholds are compared to pestilence, parasites and leeches that latch on to the mind and feed and suck the very life out of your soul. They keep you confused and isolated. These pests make you weak while they grow strong. If left unchecked, they will kill you, and try to kill whoever is around you in the process. Strong delusions create snares to keep you off focus until it is too late. You're making negative choices which come back to haunt you later.

The only way to rid yourself of the pestilence that plague the mind and emotion is treatment and pretreatment. The treatment is prayer along with the word of God. Pretreatment consist of the same exact formula. Most important, God's prescribed medicine must be mixed with faith.

To be cont'd

December 28

II Corinthians 10:3-5

"Pulling down strongholds"

Ignorance is the source of a negative stronghold. Satan has used the ignorance of God's love as a tool against the lost and saved alike. God's ways are higher than our ways. He is omnipresent. He is everywhere at one time. Anyone who calls Him, he hears. He is all-knowing. He knew what you needed before you ever asked. He can always hear you. You are always #1 on His agenda. He never sleeps. You can always rest in the fact that you are top priority. All He asks is that you seek His face - to seek after Him.

You can come before Him boldly because of the finished work of Jesus Christ. This is good news because there is nothing you can ever do to keep you away from the love of God.

To be cont'd

December 29

II Corinthians 10:3-5

"Pulling down strongholds"

If your family members have told you are dumb and will never amount to anything, when you accept this lie into your thought process, it has taken hold on your mind as well as your life. It will then attract those same kinds of thoughts to make itself stronger. Where there is unity, there is strength. Before you know it those strongholds are in your voice, your posture and your eyes.

This is why it is so important to remind yourself that your strength is from the Lord and you are made in His image. The Spirit that dwells within you does not fail.

(Luke 11:21-23) When a strong man armed keeps his palace, his goods are in peace: But when a stronger than he shall come upon him, and overcome him, he takes from him all his armor wherein he trusted, and divides his spoils.

December 30

Matthew 20:16

"The last shall be first and the first last."

The laborers set their own price. Those who serve the Lord leaving size of reward up to Him will always be given more than if they insist on knowing how much he's paid beforehand.

(Matthew 20:13) "But he answered one of them saying Friend I do you no wrong, didn't you agree with me for a penny?"

It is better to work or be used of God from the heart.

Eyes have not seen how He's able to pay. More than you could imagine!

December 31

Psalms 34:1

"I will bless the Lord at all times; his praise shall continually be in my mouth."

Make the devil do your bidding by making him your alarm clock.

When he reminds you of that person who hurt you, say, "Oh it's time to pray for them."

When he says you can't it's time to praise God.

When addiction tries to take hold, Praise the Lord.

If fear or depression tries to take root, let him know what time it is.

He will have to flee. He cannot stand your Praise.

Thoughts

365 REASONS TO STAND TALL

I hope that you have been blessed by this devotional and that they have encouraged you to know who you are – enabling you to stand tall!

Worry can become sin, if not careful, because it is a form of unbelief, but can also become a disease and is foolish for a Child of God since it's not necessary.

Worries are real but that's what makes them so dangerous.

It's foolish to worry when we can give it to the Lord. Just knowing someone cares is often the first step toward curing worry.

Today is the Tomorrow you worried about yesterday!

Remember that you are the child of a King and as such, you have …

The Right To Be Regal.

*"After all these things
do the Gentiles seek
your heavenly Father
know that ye have need
of all these things."*
Matthew 6:32

About the Author

Wanda Harper is a mom, author, child of a King and advocate for those who are less fortunate. Her nonprofit, Secret Angels, is dedicated to helping others anonymously in hopes that they will see God and not her. Her soon-to-be released cookbook, The Empty Belly Cookbook will help her fund activities for Secret Angels as well as her ministry, Feed My Sheep. You may learn more about these charitable organizations by visiting her website at

http://butterflytypefaceimw.wix.com/wharper

References

King James Bible

https://bible.org/article/names-god

http://blogs.blueletterbible.org/blb/2012/0
7/27/the-names-of-god-jehovah-rapha/

The Butterfly Typeface Publishing

The Butterfly Typeface is full service professional and writing company. Our goal is to 'spread a message' of inspiration, imagination and intrigue in all that we do. Whether you hire us to edit, ghostwrite, publish (books & magazines) or web design, you can be guaranteed exemplary customer service, fairness and quality. Our vision, under God's leadership, is to serve and assist in the healing of the heart, mind and soul of *all* people we encounter with integrity, intentional influence and positive purpose.

Iris M Williams/Owner

PO BOX 56193
Little Rock AR 72115
501-681-0080
Butterflytypeface.imw@gmail.com

WWW.BUTTERFLYTYPEFACE.COM

"We make good great!"